Journal of Educational and Psychological Consultation

Volume 13, Number 1&2

SPECIAL ISSUE
Training in Consultation: State of the Field*
Issue Editors: Judith L. Alpert and Shilpa R. Taufique

*This issue was accepted and prepared under the Editorship of Joseph E. Zins.

First published 2002 by Lawrence Erlbaum Associates, Inc.

2 Park Square, Milton Park, Abingdon, Oxfordshire OX14 4RN
52 Vanderbilt Avenue, New York, NY 10017

Routledge is an imprint of the Taylor & Francis Group, an informa business

First issued in hardback 2019

This journal is abstracted or indexed in *Exceptional Child Education Resources; Family & Society Studies Worldwide (online and CD-ROM); IFI/Ple-
num: Mental Health Abstracts; Inventory of Marriage & Family Literature; ISI:
Current Contents/Social & Behavioral Sciences, Social Sciences Citation Index,
Research Alert, Social SciSearch; Linguistics and Language Behavior Abstracts;
PsycINFO/Psychological Abstracts; Sociology of Education Abstracts; Social Services Abstracts.*

ISBN 13: 978-0-8058-9636-7 (pbk)
ISBN 13: 978-1-138-46600-5 (hbk)
ISSN 1047-4412.

Printed in the United Kingdom
by Henry Ling Limited

JOURNAL OF EDUCATIONAL AND PSYCHOLOGICAL CONSULTATION, 13(1&2), 1–3

INCOMING EDITOR'S COMMENTS

The Consultation Legacy in the *Journal of Educational and Psychological Consultation*

Emilia C. Lopez
Editor
Queens College, City University of New York

I begin my editorship in the 12th year of this journal, following the very capable footsteps of Howard Margolis and Joseph E. Zins. Howard Margolis envisioned and created the journal in 1990. Joseph E. Zins began his tenure in 1996 and ends his duties as editor with this excellent special issue focused on training in consultation.

The legacy of consultation continues with a talented the *Journal of Educational and Psychological Consultation* (*JEPC*) Editorial Review Board. The members of the review board are distinguished scholars, researchers, and practitioners with a wide range of experiences and areas of expertise in consultation. Although the new review board is being introduced in this issue, I wanted to acknowledge them for their work and contributions during the Summer and Fall of 2000, which is when I began to take over the editorial responsibilities for *JEPC*.

I also want to take the opportunity to introduce you to *JEPC*'s Associate Editors. Like the members of the editorial board, they assumed their duties in the Summer of 2000. Dr. Sylvia Rosenfield (University of Maryland in College Park) and Dr. Jan E. Hasbrouck (Texas A & M University) work with me on an ongoing basis in the process of sending out manuscripts for review and providing feedback to contributors. Dr. Kathleen C. Harris (Arizona State University West) and I collaborate in conceptualizing and editing special issues. Three associate editors are in charge of the columns featured in *JEPC*: Dr. Clyde Crego (Book and Material Reviews column), Dr. Mary M. Clare[1] (Diversity in Consultation column), and Dr. Margaret Rogers (Consultant's Corner column). Dr. Joseph E. Zins continues to work with us during our transition period in his role as mentor and advisor. I have been working with this talented group of professionals for sometime now and want to express my gratitude for their commitment, energy, and continued support.

I have a number of goals to accomplish during my term as editor. In the spirit of collaboration, I would like to encourage review board members, contributors, practitioners, scholars, and researchers to communicate your ideas, interests, and opinions regarding the scientific and practical issues that should be addressed in the journal. The legacy of consultation must continue in *JEPC* through ongoing collaboration and sharing, which are some of the basic ingredients in successful consultations. Our editorial team is committed to continuing to publish manuscripts that advance the practice and research in consultation. We intend to accomplish that goal by seeking out and accepting manuscripts that are conceptual, research-based as well as exploratory in nature. Manuscripts based on research investigations using a variety of experimental and quasiexperimental methodologies are welcomed. Qualitative instigations following the traditions of case study, ethnography, grounded theory, action research, content analysis, and discourse analysis are also encouraged.

You will see some new features in the journal. At least once a year, the journal will feature a minitheme. Minithemes will publish two to three research articles contrasting specific aspects of consultation. The articles will be accompanied by invited commentaries from experts in the consultation arena. The minithemes will also feature general articles and column articles, unlike the special issues which will be entirely devoted to individual topics that are broader in nature. Periodically, the journal will also feature interdisciplinary dialogues where consultants from a variety of disciplines, models, and orientations will have the opportunity to explore, compare, and contrast their views about research and practice in consultation. The next issue of the journal will debut the Diversity in Consultation column, edited by Dr. Mary M. Clare. The Diversity in Consultation column will provide a forum for short articles that explore issues of human diver-

---

[1]Mary Henning-Stout has legally changed her name to Mary M. Clare.

sity in consultation including culture, language, ethnicity, sexual orientation, and religion. (A statement of purpose for that column will be featured in Volume 13, Issue 3).

Some familiar features remain in the journal. The manuscripts published in *JEPC* will continue to maintain an interdisciplinary perspective by publishing the work of consultants from many different fields. Special issues will be published at least two times a year focusing on a variety of topics. The Consultant's Corner and Book and Materials Reviews column will also continue.

As I officially begin my editorial responsibilities, I thank the Lawrence Erlbaum Associates, Inc. staff for their support. In advance, my thanks to the Associate Editors and members of the Editorial Review Board for their contributions, collegiality, and feedback during my editorial term. I feel honored to work with such an excellent group of professionals and for having the opportunity to continue the legacy of consultation in *JEPC*.

JOURNAL OF EDUCATIONAL AND PSYCHOLOGICAL CONSULTATION, 13(1&2), 5–6

OUTGOING EDITOR'S FAREWELL

Building a Strong Future for Educational and Psychological Consultation

Joseph E. Zins
University of Cincinnati

This issue of the *Journal of Educational and Psychological* addresses a major need in the field, that is, the training of professionals in education and psychology for a consultative role. The guest editors, Judith Alpert and Shilpa Taufique, have done an outstanding job of assembling a diverse group of new and very experienced experts to share their perspectives on this topic. The candor with which the contributors discuss the topic should be enlightening to all of us.

In many ways this issue symbolizes the overall consultation field. It is encouraging to see how the field continues to develop, how consultation has become an important role for many professionals, and how practice is becoming more scientifically based. Disciplines such as school psychology and special education especially have been in the forefront in developing the field, although their work has not been widely disseminated to other areas such as clinical psychology, counseling, speech and language pathology, and industrial–organizational psychology, that engage in much consultation practice and thus could benefit from this knowledge base.

The scientific advances the field has made are important, and as is commonly acknowledged, there continues to be a need for more of it. At the same time, attention needs to be given to making the research more useful. For example, adoption of consistent terminology will make it far easier to draw conclusions and make generalizations. Yet, there is a propensity for the field to invent new terms for concepts that already are in existence. Similarly, although researchers recognize that it is important to build on the ideas of previous studies, there is a concurrent responsibility to acquire a thorough knowledge of the literature, yet it is common to cite only the most recent publications. Furthermore, imagine how the field could develop if there was more consistency across studies with respect to how implementation quality is measured, what outcomes are examined, and in the measurement instruments that are used.

There clearly is much to be done to advance the field. Addressing the concerns raised will require increased communication and agreement among those involved in this work. And, because training in consultation is the key to much of this research, the recommendation of Hellkamp, Zins, Ferguson, and Hodge (1998) that another national conference on consultation be held needs to be pursued. The 1980s saw some major steps forward following the National Conference on Consultation Training at McGill University in 1980 (Alpert & Meyers, 1983), and perhaps some similar movement might occur if leading researchers and practitioners from diverse fields involved in consultation were convened.

ACKNOWLEDGMENTS

This is my last issue as Editor of *JEPC*, so it is time to pass the baton to Dr. Emilia Lopez. I wish her much success, and I hope she finds the experience as fulfilling as I have. It has been a true privilege to serve in this role. I have had an opportunity to interact and learn from so many smart and creative individuals over the last 6 years. It has been my pleasure to work with a team of talented Associate Editors. I'm especially appreciative of Tim Heron, Maurice Elias, Kathy Harris, and Howard Margolis, who have served in this capacity since I began my term; I am grateful for their many professional contributions, their support, and their friendship. The many members of the Editorial Review Board likewise have helped to make this a quality journal. Finally, I wish to thank my partner, Charlene R. Ponti, Ph.D., and our wonderful children, Lauren, Michael, and Ryan, for keeping me focused on what's most important in life.

REFERENCES

Alpert, J.L., & Meyers, J. (Eds.).(1983). *Training in consultation*. Springfield, IL: Thomas.
Hellkamp, D.T., Zins, J.E., Ferguson, K., & Hodge, M. (1998). Training practices in consultation: A national survey of clinical, counseling, industrial/organizational, and school psychology faculty. *Consulting Psychology Journal: Practice and Research, 50,* 228-236.

JOURNAL OF EDUCATIONAL AND PSYCHOLOGICAL CONSULTATION, 13(1&2), 7–11

SPECIAL ISSUE
INTRODUCTION

Consultation Training: A Field in Need of Review, Revision, and Research

Judith L. Alpert and Shilpa R. Taufique
New York University

A basic premise underlying this volume is that the field of consultation training needs review, revision, research, and a continuing focus to further develop the professional practice of consultation. This special issue considers the consultation training literature and the state of consultation training. In addition, it exemplifies some issues that are presently being conceptualized within consultation training as well as some areas in need of research and additional conceptualization. I hope this volume will stimulate research and thinking about consultation training.

This issue considers topics that have received relatively little attention in the literature. In addition, the introductory and concluding sections point to some parameters, concerns, questions, and themes relevant to future consultation training and consultation training research.

The contributors vary in orientation (mental health, behavioral, organizational, instructional, or a combination of these). For a consideration of definitions, theoretical bases and assumptions underlying the definition, goals, participants and roles, methods of instruction, and limitations of

Correspondence should be addressed to Judith L. Alpert, New York University, 239 Greene Street, Fifth Floor, New York, NY 10003. E-mail: judie.alpert@nyu.edu

some consultation orientations, the reader is referred to Meyers, Alpert, and Fleisher (1983). In general, there is little communication between consultants who differ in orientation. Nevertheless, there are common problems, issues, questions, and dilemmas facing consultation trainers across orientations. Articles in this special issue make this clear. Most of the authors are university-based trainers and consultants, and many have written extensively in the area of consultation. Several have been teaching consultation for decades. All the authors hold that consultation should play a major role in the delivery of services, are concerned about the lack of research and writing in consultation training, are committed to the study of the consultation process as well as the consultation training process, and contend that there is a need to evaluate consultation training as well as a need to describe training. In addition, most of the contributors have grounded their work in Caplan's model of mental health consultation.

The authors consider process and content of either inservice or preservice consultation training. In general, they have considered the following with respect to the general topic of consultation training:

1. What are the limitations of the consultation training literature?
2. What should be considered in either inservice or preservice consultation training?
3. What are some unanswered questions in regard to consultation training?
4. What are implications for research in consultation training?

Some questions which continue to be raised include: in which orientation (mental health, behavioral, organizational, instructional, or a combination of these) should individuals be trained? Is it possible to train students in all the orientations? When should consultation training occur? What is the best means of providing supervision? The questions are numerous.

In the article titled "Expanding Problem Solving Consultation Training: Prospects and Frameworks," Kratochwill and Pittman focus on the content of what needs to be considered in behavioral consultation training. They label their version of behavioral consultation "problem-solving consultation," and provide a conceptual framework for what a curriculum in the behavioral–problem-solving model would be at both the preservice and inservice levels. In thinking about prospective consultation training, Kratochwill and Pittman extend the domains of what is traditionally considered consultation. Underlying this article is the belief that behavioral–problem-solving consultation needs to be expanded in its conceptual base, and that this expansion has direct implications for the content of consultation training. Specifically they note that the scope of what is considered consultation and the core concepts that have traditionally been linked primarily to case-centered consultation demand examination. In addition, they provide a context for their framework by means of a brief review of the literature on training behavioral consultants.

There are similarities between behavioral and instructional consultation. The focus of Rosenfield's article is on training instructional consultants. As Rosenfield indicates, while behavioral and mental health consultation are the most common, instructional consultation is the third most common model of consultation taught in school psychology training programs. Rosenfield is concerned about inservice training. However, in this article, her focus is on preservice education for graduate students in school psychology, school counseling, and special education. She identifies what is important in training instructional consultants and provides a framework for such education. She holds that the instructional consultant, in addition to knowing the fundamental components of instructional consultation, must have a conceptual model for skill development. Rosenfield is the architect of instructional consultation. She holds that instructional consultation, which is a form of consultee-centered consultation, is a stage-based problem-solving process that is dependent on communication and good working relationships. It has an ecological stance and a focus that is on academic and behavioral concerns in school settings. Rosenfield identifies the levels of development in consultation training. In the first stage, there is development of conceptual understanding and some skills. With supervised application of skills in school settings, competency may be realized. Rosenfield indicates that instructional consultation supervision must focus on relationship issues, language, and content, and involves the audiotaping of consultation sessions for training purposes. To achieve expertise in instructional consultation, she advocates for extended opportunities for practice, supervision and research. She concludes her article with a consideration of implications for consultation practice and a recognition of the need for organized inservice training.

Inservice training is the focus of the article by Gravois, Babinski, and Knotek. In "Educating Practitioners as Consultants: Development and Evaluation of the Instructional Consultation Team Consortium," they describe a comprehensive, statewide effort to systematically train a diverse group of educational practitioners as instructional consultants within the context of a team service delivery model. In addition, they describe their effort and summarize the empirically based professional development process used to support practitioners' consultation skill development and use, and they present the results of a retrospective pretest survey that constitutes the evaluation of the impact of this continuing education approach.

The most pragmatic articles in this special issue are those by J. Meyers, Alpert and Taufique, and A. Meyers. In these articles, they consider how they conceptualize their courses and address some issues around course organization, dilemmas, and questions. J. Meyers considers questions about the content of consultation training in "A 30 Year Perspective on Best Practices for Consultation Training." In addition, J. Meyers considers linking theory to practice as well as other challenges in consultation training such as amount of autonomy appropriate for trainees, multicultural issues, and the timing of consultation education within preservice level training. Suggestions for training are derived from a model of mental health consultation and consultation training. The model adopts psychodynamic, cognitive or behavioral, and ecological principles within a constructivist framework, is empowerment oriented, and focuses on cultivating the trainee's continuous practice of consultation. J. Meyers highlights the need for research on consultation training. In addition, he proposes the adoption of a practitioner–researcher stance in which practicing consultants consider themselves researchers who share their practice data with other school-based consultants and, in this way, contribute to a developing knowledge base. J. Meyers concludes with directions for researching the process and outcome of consultation training.

Alpert and Taufique focus on selected aspects of conceptualizing a consultation training experience. First, Alpert and Taufique provide a historical consideration of consultation training. They review and place into historical perspective the limited consultation training literature. They describe the two-semester consultation practicum course at New York University to provide background for a consideration of three precourse questions. Pragmatic issues are the focus of the majority of the article titled "Consultation Training: 26 Years and Three Questions." The three questions are: (1) What criteria should be used in selecting a consultation placement? (2) What criteria should be used in selecting a field supervisor? (3) What criteria should be used in evaluating the work of the consultants in the consultation course? Alpert and Taufique use a case example in synergy with these questions. Like Rosenfield, and Alpert and Taufique consider the issue of supervision. They indicate that little has been written about supervision with respect to consultation training. Alpert and Taufique make the point that there are no full resolutions to these precourse questions. Rather, they speak of evolving answers. While relevant literature is reviewed, it is grounded in the interaction between the first author's 26 years of teaching a 1-year long practicum course on school consultation and the second author's experience as a novice consultant and consultant trainer "in-utero." Alpert and Taufique conclude by identifying implications for training and research.

A different perspective is offered by A. Meyers in her article titled "Developing Nonthreatening Expertise: Thought on Consultation Training From the Perspective of a New Faculty Member." A. Meyers is a recent graduate of a doctoral program in clinical-community psychology, a new professor in a school psychology program, and a first-time instructor of a consultation course. She describes her experiences teaching consultation for the first time. Specifically, she considers how she planned the course and managed some initial dilemmas and challenges. Some of the issues she considered include means of adapting the consultation course into the broader school psychology training program, determining the allocation of didactic and applied training course components, and teaching effective collaboration. A. Meyers has found the work of sociologist Patricia Collins helpful in conceptualizing the meaning of expertise from a collaborative point of view. A. Meyers holds that collaboration involves the ability to recognize and appreciate expertise in oneself and others. She believes that trainees need to develop increasing comfort with their own expert knowledge as well as to learn to respect the expertise of consultees. Thus, she works toward helping trainees develop into nonthreatening experts. She concludes by calling for research on the contribution of epistemological theory to consultation training and practice.

Terry Gutkin, the discussant, closes the special issue by discussing the articles, suggesting future directions, and marking a research agenda for consultation training. What this issue makes clear is that there remains much to understand, clarify, and pass on.

REFERENCES

Meyers, J., Alpert, J. L., & Fleisher, B. D. (1983). Models of consultation. In J. L. Alpert & J. Meyers (Eds.), *Training in consultation: Perspectives from mental health, behavioral, and organizational consultation* (pp. 5–14). Springfield, IL: Thomas.

Judith L. Alpert is Professor of Applied Psychology at New York University. Her research interests include: child sexual abuse, date and acquaintance violence, school violence, and prevention.

Shilpa Taufique, M.A. is a doctoral candidate at New York University. Her research interests include: consultation, relation between culture and child abuse, school violence, and prevention.

JOURNAL OF EDUCATIONAL AND PSYCHOLOGICAL CONSULTATION, 13(1&2), 13–33
Copyright © 2002, Lawrence Erlbaum Associates, Inc.

Consultation Training:
26 Years and Three Questions

Judith L. Alpert and Shilpa R. Taufique
New York University

The purpose of this article is to further graduate-level training in school consultation. Three questions that the first author has encountered throughout the last 26 years while teaching consultation are illuminated in this article: (1) What criteria should be used in selecting a consultation placement? (2) What criteria should be used in selecting a field supervisor? (3) What criteria should be used in evaluating the work of the consultants in the consultation course? Placing these questions into currency in the school psychology training literature may ensue more thinking around these critical issues. A case example provided by the second author is used in synergy with the questions and serves to expound on them.

The first author's "consultation birth date" is 1975, when she began teaching a two-semester practicum course in school consultation. The first author is happy to report that she is 26 "consultation years old." Presently, the second author is in "consultation-utero" as an advanced student at New York University.

The first author's gestation period began in 1969, when she was a PhD candidate in School Psychology and while she was doing a clinical-community internship at Seymour Sarason's Yale University Psycho-Educational Clinic. Whereas her internship focused on consultation, she had never taken a course in it. In fact, few training programs in School Psychology were offering courses in school consultation at that time and, to the authors' knowledge, no programs were offering a two-semester practicum

Correspondence should be addressed to Judith L. Alpert, New York University, Department of Applied Psychology, 239 Greene Street, 5th Floor, New York, NY 10003. E-mail: judie.alpert@nyu.edu

course in school consultation in 1975. As Rosenfield indicates in this volume, presently few school psychology programs offer more than one semester of school consultation training.

In the 60s, there was very little written about consultation. The consultation literature at the time primarily emphasized the use of a medical model through which diagnoses of problems would be made and treatment would be delivered (Hitchcock & Mooney, 1969; Toenes, Lytle, Wagner, & Wimberger, 1968; Williams, 1967). Much of the early consultation literature focused on the delivery of indirect services by psychiatrists to schools (Adams & Weinick, 1966; Caplan, 1970; Loomis, 1966; Mariner, Brandt, Stone, & Mirmow, 1961; Millar, 1966; Shearer, 1968; Sussman & Zimberg, 1967; Westman, 1968) and to community agencies (Greenberg et al., 1958; Lifschutz, Stewart, & Harrison, 1958; Maddux, 1953). Only a few authors (e.g., Canter & Feder, 1968; Libo, 1996; Newman, 1967; Sarason, 1966) discussed the use of consultation by clinical and community psychologists to provide indirect service in varied settings. There was little, if anything written about consultation by school psychologists at that time. While there was a great deal of excitement about indirect service delivery, our understanding of the practice of School Psychology at that time was that few school psychologists actually engaged in doing consultation.

Immediately after the first author completed her year of internship, she began to consult in schools and, a few years later, she was born—consultatively, that is. Alpert began to teach consultation in the School Psychology program at New York University in 1975. While J. Meyers (this issue), and perhaps others, taught a one-semester practicum course in school consultation at that time, Alpert did not know anyone who taught a two-semester practicum course. Thus, she struggled with its development.

Since the 1960s, the literature on consultation has expanded considerably. However, with respect to consultation training, the literature is relatively deficient. There are some sources in the clinical, community, and school psychology literature that describe and evaluate various consultation training models and programs (Gallessich, Long, & Jennings, 1986; Hellkamp, Zins, Ferguson, & Hodge, 1998; Meyers, 1984; Meyers, Wurtz, & Flanagan, 1981; Zins, 1989). Much of the literature describes training in behavioral consultation (Kratochwill & Bergen, 1978; Kratochwill, Sheridan, Carrington-Rotto, & Salmon, 1992; Kratochwill & Van Someren, 1984; Sheridan, 1997; Sheridan, Salmon, Kratochwill, & Carrington-Rotto, 1992). Others address the use of different perspectives in training, such as systems theory (Harper & Spellman, 1994; Van Velsor & Cox, 2000) and mental health consultation (Berlin, 2001; Caplan & Caplan, 1993; Peebles & O'Malley, 1978; Pinkerton & Temple, 2000). However, references concerning field placement selection, supervisor selection, and trainee evaluation are rare.

In this article, we consider the course developed by Alpert in mental health consultation and organizational development. The model of the course, based on the models of Caplan (1970), Sarason (1966), and Newman (1967), combines the depth of a psychodynamic approach with the breadth of a more social psychological approach. Although the focus in the first and second semesters of the course is more on mental health or organizational development respectively, it is a flexible model, which is responsive to system needs. The course provides knowledge of various consultation perspectives through training in the four theoretical orientations (behavioral, mental health, organizational development, advocacy). Recommendations for training in all four orientations can be found throughout the consultation training literature (Gallessich et al., 1986; Meyers, 1984).Three precourse questions are considered in this discussion. The intent is to place these questions into currency within the consultation training literature. At the outset, it should be clear that there are no full resolutions at the present time. We call the answers "partial answers" because they are evolving.

TWO-SEMESTER PRACTICUM COURSE

As described elsewhere (Alpert, Feit, & Grant, 1983; Alpert & Paulson, 1990; Alpert, Silverstein, & Haynes, 1980), students in the school psychology program at NYU are required to take the two-semester, year-long practicum course in their second year of training. The course, taught by the first author, usually has 12–15 students. For purposes of this article, the consultation students will be called "consultants," and the clients (children) in those schools in which they consult will be called "students." The graduate assistant for the course reads and comments on some of the written work; works closely with the consultants on developing and maintaining consultative relationships with administration, staff, and students in field settings; supervises consultants weekly in small groups; and is supervised by the course instructor on all of the previous. For 2 years Taufique, the second author, served as the graduate assistant for the course.

In conjunction with the practicum course, consultants are placed in a field setting, usually a school, for a minimum of one day (PhD students) to three days (PsyD students) per week. The course is designed to prepare trainees to help (a) individual teachers and other staff function more effectively with children and youth, and (b) teachers and administrators function more effectively with each other. Consultants are assigned readings on such topics as school culture, entry, systems theory, participant observation, history and theory of consultation, principles of prevention, processes of change, models of consultation, and the implementation and evaluation of programs.

Each consultant applies consultation skills by developing a program specific to the needs of their settings. At one time, Alpert encouraged the consultants to develop child sexual abuse prevention programs. More recently, Alpert and Taufique urged the development of various violence prevention programs and especially adolescent acquaintance and date violence prevention programs. When consultants develop prevention projects in the same area, such as violence or child sexual abuse prevention, they can share resources. In general, the projects give consultants an opportunity to integrate an understanding of intervention strategies and principles of planned change and prevention with the realities of the school culture, including its needs and resources. The projects involve primary, secondary, or tertiary prevention and focus on the system, parents, school staff, or students. Some of the programs focus on several or all of these levels.

In addition to readings and fieldwork, consultants write a theoretical paper and numerous logs in which they analyze their consultative and program development activity using the various theoretical perspectives learned. They have a minimum of 2 hr of weekly supervision as well, 1 hr each with their field and university supervisors. Additional supervision is provided on an as-needed basis.

THREE PRECOURSE QUESTIONS

Although the course has presented us with many questions, three in particular are singled out here. These questions arise early, before the course begins. Although there are others that present prior to the course commencing, these three were selected because they have been consistent, challenging, and representative. They are central to training in school consultation, and relevant to other types of consultation training as well. Once the course begins, the questions breed at a swift pace. Clearly, teaching consultation is a very complex business.

The three questions are: (1) What criteria should be used in *selecting a consultation placement*? (2) What criteria should be used in *selecting a field supervisor*? (3) What criteria should be used in *evaluating the work of the consultants* in the consultation course? Questions one and two are interrelated;

while sometimes one can select a supervisor from several within a placement, usually there is only one supervisor in each setting. Regarding the third criteria (evaluating the work of the consultants), it may seem curious that an end-of-course event such as evaluation is included as a precourse question. However, issues of evaluation must be determined prior to the commencement of a course and listed in the course outline.

Before considering the questions, some clarification must be made. It is acknowledged that each of the three questions could constitute an entire paper, and that each has received some attention in the general literature on training psychologists (Alpert & Meyers, 1983; Fagan & Wise, 1994; Ware & Millard, 1987). These questions are pursued here because they have received relatively little attention in the consultation training literature. Second, the intent of this article should be made clear. The intent is to place these questions into currency within the consultation training literature. It is hoped, by doing so, more thinking around these issues will ensue. Third, some license is taken in this article. While selected consultation and related literatures are considered, the article is grounded in the interaction between the first author's 26 years of teaching a 1-year long practicum course on school consultation, and the second author's experience as a novice consultant and consultation trainer "in-utero." A case example precedes a consideration of the questions and will be used in synergy with them. The example illustrates the situation Taufique, as a novice consultant, faced at the beginning of her second year of graduate training when she was a student in Alpert's course in school consultation. The case is intricate and raises multifarious issues for the consultant, many of which are perplexing and profound. Given space limitations, only those aspects of the case that are most relevant to the questions will be considered. Also, some alterations were made and some parallel phenomena have been created. In some cases, several individuals were merged into one. These alterations were made to protect the confidentiality of those involved, and should not diminish an understanding about schools, consultation experience, and the process of learning to be a consultant.

Case Example

The small junior high school in New York City in which the consultant was placed served students who were mostly from single parent families of low socioeconomic status. Many of the students had traumatic histories of loss, abuse, and neglect. Inappropriate sexual behavior was rampant in the school and was occurring among the 11–15 year olds in the hallways, classrooms, and schoolyard. The consultant was faced with some explicit stories of sexual harassment between students as well as sexual subjugation of some female staff by some male students. Also, the consultant heard about sexual activity between students outside of school, only some of which was consensual. Inappropriate sexual behavior was the norm in and outside of this school. What was missing was an *understanding* of the behavior, how it could occur, why it was not dealt with by school personnel or other authorities, and how it could best be addressed.

Several school factors are of relevance. Administrative focus on and support around this issue was nonexistent. While the students were divided into victims or perpetrators, it was clear that they were all victims of a situation in which no one seemed to know how to secure safety, direction, or order. The principal had an overpowering and negative presence within this school, which often resulted in conflict among staff, administration, and students. Not surprisingly, teachers did not stay in this adverse environment for long. In fact, none of the teachers had been at the school longer than 2 years. How did teachers deal with the inappropriate sexual tumults? They followed the administrative lead and either ignored the sexual behavior of the students or joked about it. Stated simply, they were "clueless" as to how to proceed.

A specific incident is telling. A 13-year old girl was sexually assaulted in a public park by five of her male classmates during the end of the prior school year. The assault was one horrifying half-hour long incident, which involved fondling by all five boys while the girl was physically restrained. After the girl's parents called the police, two of the offenders were sent to juvenile detention for several months before they were transferred to another school. The other three offenders were placed on probation and sentenced to community service for several months.

When the next school year began, the victimized girl and the three offending boys were once again in the same grade and in all the same classes. Students in the classes knew of the assault and the aftermath. Many were anxious. There was an epidemic of gossiping, whispering, and nervous laughter. Some of the staff and students blamed the victim for the events. In and out of school, she was the target of verbal abuse and angry acts of revenge. She was called the "school slut."

Her friends darted from standing by their friend to protecting their own reputations. Both female friends and enemies were afraid that they, too, would be assaulted and would become a continual target for abuse. The students were well aware that their teachers and school administrators were not assuming a protective role. They were frightened.

Whereas the students thought the teachers did not care, the consultant *knew* that the teachers were frightened. They did not know what to do. They were more intent on somehow finishing the school year and finding a better placement for the following year than dealing with what they perceived to be an overwhelming and hopeless situation.

Thus, this was a school in which there were few limits. Some students were out of control. Many were scared. Chaos was rampant. It appeared that no one knew how to gain control. No one had the energy or commitment to try to gain it. No one had the belief that it was possible to garner command.

The school had an on-site psychologist, who was the consultant's field supervisor. She too, had a "hands off" response to the rampant sexual events and she demanded the same of the consultant. While there were many organizational problems, the psychologist avoided intervention at the organizational level. In addition, the principal and the psychologist (consultant's on-site supervisor) chose not to work together. They did not like each other. Given her association to the psychologist, the principal seemed to avoid contact with the consultant, and the psychologist encouraged the consultant to do the same. This was the situation that the novice consultant faced at the beginning of her second year of graduate training.

It is important to point out that this situation is not unique to New York City or unique to families that have endured traumatic histories. In fact, a recent article in the New York Times (Goode, 2001) supports previous research and indicates that, in a dating relationship, one in five adolescent girls become the victim of physical or sexual violence or both. Specifically, approximately 20% of the 14–18 year old girls in the study of over 2000 girls reported that they had been hit, slapped, shoved or forced into sexual activity by a dating partner. While these events are relatively common, there is little within the consultation literature about how to consult around such events.

Selecting a Consultation Placement: A Collage of Placements

The School Psychology program at New York University has engaged a full-time university staff member who takes responsibility for the selection of placements and the match between them and the consultants. Thus, faculty are less involved with this issue at present. Nevertheless, the issue of placement selection is a complex and important issue that demands attention.

There are many criteria that could be used in selecting consultation placements for training purposes. The general literature on training psychologists makes some reference to selection of field placements that could apply to consultation training as well (Alpert & Meyers, 1983; Crespi & Lopez, 1998; Ehly et al., 1987; Fagan & Wise, 1994). Some of the criteria mentioned include practicum objectives and training responsibilities; supervision quality; supervisory evaluations (Crespi & Lopez, 1998); supervisor/supervisee theoretical orientation; trainee's level of competence (Putney, Worthington, & McCullough, 1992); number of field supervisors; and ranges of ages, grade levels, and populations served (Alessi, Lascurettes-Alessi, & Leys, 1981). However, although many of the issues that arise in training psychologists in general are applicable to consultation training, Atella and Figgatt (1998) noted that there are several issues unique to consultation practicum training.

Over the years, pragmatism has played a role in the selection of placements. For example, one criterion is accessibility. There is an interest in schools that afford easy access to consultants. The training and consultation skill of the supervisor is another issue that is considered. Other important factors involve the consultants and include balancing such issues as the match between consultants' learning needs and placement contribution, and the match between consultants' skills and placement needs. Selection of placements is a sophisticated activity.

Other criteria focus on diversity. For example, within any year, the goal is to have the consultants' placements within the class to be diverse from each other with respect to such variables as level of school (nursery, elementary, junior high school, high school), size of school, type of school (private or public, religious or nonreligious, etc.), population served (special needs), type and availability of school services, types of problems schools present, and receptivity to consultation. The design is to maximize the range of experience of the consultants. Having students work in schools that differ from each other on many dimensions as well as having students discuss their placements and these differences in class results in the consultants having a broad experience.

Hence, *a collage of placements* is envisioned. Each selected placement must have something unique to offer to the consultants in the class. While each consultant is actually in one setting only, collectively the consultants in the class learn about the personalities and characteristics of 12, if there are 12 people in the class. Thus, for example, they learn about consulting in a school in which the fieldwork supervisor does not work well with the principal as well as about a school in which she does. Through class discussion, they learn more about how to deal with this situation.

They learn about a school, for example, in which there is much receptivity to consultation and they learn about a school in which the staff know little about consultation and are most resistant to it. The consultants have an opportunity to learn about many placements and different issues that may be endemic to various settings. Thus, they have knowledge of 12–15 placements rather than merely the one that their placement affords. This format also encourages consultants to develop and maintain peer groups where they can share knowledge, provide support, engage in collaborative problem solving, and foster professional growth. The value of professional peer groups in consultation has been described elsewhere (Zins & Murphy, 1996).

Having consultants buy into this *"collage of placements"* model, however, is a difficult charge. Consider the previous case example, which presents multifarious and complex problems involving rampant inappropriate sexual bedlam, out-of-control student behavior, scared students and staff, and prevailing chaos. There was no support or limit setting by the psychologist, administration, or other authorities with respect to the sexual bedlam. It was a situation in which it appeared that no one knew how to gain control and no one had the energy or commitment to try to gain it or the belief that it was possible. This was the situation Taufique faced when she was barely 1 month into our year long course. She knew little about consultative theory or practice. She did not have process skills and knowledge. Needless to say, this was a very difficult situation, and presents a challenge to even the most seasoned school consultant. Perhaps not surprisingly, some students might wish for a different placement. In this case, the consultant welcomed the challenge. Although she might have preferred a more gradual introduction to the complexities of consultation over the convoluted arrangement, she was inspired by the opportunity to present material in class, which provided a dramatic opportunity for learning about such issues as establishing priorities, planning and time perspective, challenging and consulting with supervisors, utilizing resources outside the school, implementing school programs, and intervening at an organizational level in a school, which was initially against and skeptical of such intervention.

Also, she had a context in which to understand her placement. She knew she was dealing with a difficult situation as did her fellow students. The other consultants supported her while, at the same time, they exposed her to other consultative experiences. In addition, by hearing about many different experiences, each consultant could place their consultative experience in perspective.

Alpert, Weiner, and Ludwig's (1979) research is relevant here. To learn more about how content of change, degree of change, and initial level of functioning influence consultants' evaluation of consultation outcome, 14 mental health consultants completed a questionnaire. For each of the 18 pre–post consultation ratings on the questionnaire (2 content × 3 degree of change × 3 initial levels = 18), consultants rated the success of consultation and the degree to which they would like to have been the consultant. Analysis of variance results for both dependent measures indicated main effects for degree of change and initial level. Neither main effects for content nor interaction effects were indicated. It appeared that consultants perceived consultation as more successful with and preferred working with consultees who improved the most and who *function at a higher initial level*. The finding that degree of change influenced evaluation of outcome is not surprising. It seems reasonable that amount of improvement would determine how consultation is evaluated. The finding that initial level of functioning influences evaluation of outcome is more surprising. It appears that relatively inexperienced consultants evaluate consultative interventions more positively when they work with consultees who function initially at a higher level.

Consistent with this finding, in another study Alpert, Ludwig, and Weiner (1979) found that teacher–consultees most in need of assistance are not selected for consultation, and that the most preferred teacher–consultees, in comparison to least preferred teacher–consultees, are perceived as less needy of assistance around issues concerning children and lessons, more responsive to consultation, and more likable. It appears that teachers most in need of assistance are not selected for consultation. It may be that schools most in need are not selected as well. By utilizing the "collage of placements" model, we are able to select such schools in need that are typically neglected. In doing so, consultants have the opportunity to broaden their experiences and their understandings of how applying theory to practice can be a complicated task. At the same time, the schools are able to receive much needed services. In some cases, exposure to such difficult placements serves as a valuable educational experience for novice consultants who, as a result of such exposure, may eventually be better equipped to serve such challenging settings.

Thus, we have adopted a "collage of placements" model. Some consultants consult in schools in which there is less need and there is a higher initial level of functioning while others consult in schools where there is more need and a lower initial level of functioning. Some consult in schools in which there is a great need for assistance. What facilitates their adopting the "collage of placements" model? The answer: (1) the use of class "wiselies" and (2) the means of evaluating the work of the consultants. The evaluation of the work on the consultants is discussed later in this article.

Wiselies

In almost every consultation class meeting, at least one consultant is asked to present a "wisely." Specifically, the student consultants are asked to present a particular situation that they wished they had dealt with "more wisely." They are asked to state clearly what they felt was "not wise" about what they did in their role as a consultant. Following, there is class discussion as to how the consultant could have dealt with the situation "more wisely." Usually the discussion begins with questions in an effort to understand the situation and the placement better. Later in the discussion there might be some role-playing, clarifying, elaborating, summarizing of information, or opinion giving. These may result in more questioning. The course instructor is very active in these discussions. Over time the consultants become more active. Not only are the other class members consulting with the "wisely-presenter," but they are also learning about various schools and school staff as well as consultation issues and problems. Toward the end of these wiselies we talk about what was helpful and less helpful to the presenting consultant. This provides another opportunity to learn about giving and receiving consultation, and facilitates discussion about the efficacy of the work.

Consultants are told that "wiselies" provide opportunities for learning. They are told that mistakes afford occasions for useful feedback. They are told that blunders are inevitable and necessary. "Wiselies" demonstrate that consultant's need to listen, think, and question to understand a problem. Also, they demonstrate that answers often develop slowly and that probing is an important part of the process of understanding. Thus, "wiselies" afford an opportunity to learn about different placements, problems, and issues, as well as provide an occasion to practice being a consultant under the supervision of the course instructor.

Selecting a Field Supervisor: A Collage of Supervisors

The literature on supervision addresses several issues relevant to general training in psychology. Some of the issues discussed include supervision modalities (Romans, Boswell, Carlozzi, & Ferguson, 1995; Ryan, Lombardi, Liederman, & Zelinger, 1980), supervisor and/or supervisee characteristics, and how they influence supervision (Gatmon et al., 2001; Putney et al., 1992; Robiner, Saltzman, Hoberman, Semrud-Clikeman, & Schirvar, 1998), and the importance of supervision in training (Alessi et al., 1981; Crespi & Lopez, 1998; Ross & Goh, 1993).

An example of some literature on supervision that is relevant to general training is that by Romans and colleagues (1995). They report findings from a study that considered the frequency of use for various supervisory modalities (videotape review, self-report only, live supervision, audiotape review, cotherapy). According to this study, it was found that clinical and counseling programs use videotape review most while school psychology programs use self-report most frequently. The modalities rated as having the most strength for all types of programs (clinical, counseling, and school) were, in order of strength, cotherapy as supervision, live supervision, videotape review, audiotape review, and self-report only. One question that can be raised concerns the generalizability of research on supervision in general to supervision in consultation.

While there is a literature on supervision training, there is a dearth of literature on supervision of consultation training and an even greater dearth with respect to models of consultant supervision. There is some literature, however, that delineates a model of consultation supervision that has been adapted from a model of supervision used with training counselors (Stoltenberg, 1993), and that describes a vertical supervision model (Alpert et al., 1983), which is the model utilized in the course described in this article.

The vertical supervision model was developed in response to criticism toward traditional one-to-one approaches. It is an alternate model that involves a multilevel, hierarchical arrangement of at least three levels: student supervisees, advanced student supervisors, and professional supervisors. Those at each level supervise those "beneath them" while being supervised by those "above them." Final responsibility for all levels involved lies with the person in the top hierarchical position. In the case of Alpert's consultation course, the consultants (student supervisees) are supervised by the field supervisor and the graduate assistant (advanced student supervisor), who is in turn supervised by the course professor.

This multisourced supervision received by consultants in our program presents some advantages and raises some interesting issues. One advantage is that it reduces the threat of evaluation as second year consultation students receive supervision from less threatening advanced student supervisors. Another advantage is that consultants receive input from several supervisors who may work and think differently. They are exposed to many different ways of conceptualizing issues and ways of working.

There are disadvantages as well. Being supervised by more than one supervisor can be confusing and overwhelming. The response from various supervisors may be difficult for some supervisees to integrate. Furthermore, the consultant could be in a situation in which different supervisors strongly disagree with each other. This could result in the consultant feeling ethically and morally mandated to take action in a way that contradicts direction from the field supervisor. While our aim is to place consultants with a field supervisor who demonstrates "good" consultation and who has excellent consultative relationships with school staff, we sometimes find that some of the placements lack in this as well as other regards. Over the years, there is less concern over this. What seems to result in most learning is the situation in which there is diversity across placements on many dimensions, and this includes supervisory skill and supervisor's relationships with staff. In the consultant's professional life following the consultation course, the consultant may have a less than ideal supervisor or work with a less than ideal administrator or colleague. Consultants need to learn *how* to work with different people who present with different skills. Also, they learn that they can provide *consultation to their supervisors.* Consultants in our course have supervision from the field supervisor, the graduate assistant, their peers in the consultation class, and the professor. If supervision in the field is not ideal, they can lean on classmates or university supervisors, learn how to be a consultant to *their* field supervisor, and provide the consultation class with material, which should introduce school life as it is and lead to clarification of values, advocacy, ethics, action, and learning.

In the case concerning rampant inappropriate sexual behavior, the various supervisors disagreed. The field supervisor encouraged avoiding difficult situations and the university supervisors supported the consultant in confrontation. Whose direction does the consultant follow? The field supervisor has ultimate responsibility for the work of the consultant in her setting. At the same time, each of the situations must be considered as they arise. Sometimes, when the field supervisor is presented with an alternate way of thinking, change results. Sometimes this is not the case. Regardless, the multiple inputs, as with the multiple settings in the "collage of placements," usually result in a broader and deeper conceptualization.

Evaluating the Work of the Consultants: The Three Rs and Partial Success

The literature on evaluation of trainees is similar to that on supervision of trainees. That is, there is a lack of material on evaluation of trainees within consultation training. The consultation literature includes many sources referring to the efficacy of behavioral consultation (Sheridan, 1992; Sterling-Turner, Watson, Wildmon, Watkins, & Little, 2001). The majority of the literature that considers the efficacy of consultation has focused on behavioral consultation. This may be because behavioral consultation is the more frequent model utilized. It may also be that it is taught and implemented within a structured framework and training procedures that allow for more rigorously controlled dissemination of knowledge and monitoring of training outcomes. Efficacy of consultation is typically assessed through multiple modalities (direct observation, self-report, self-monitoring, consultee report of consultation effectiveness, and formal written examinations) (Kratochwill & Van Someren, 1984). In the literature, there is little information about the evaluation of trainees who utilize models of consultation other than behavioral consultation.

At New York University, many people informally evaluate the work of the consultants: the instructor and graduate assistant, the consultants themselves, and the field supervisor. In addition, there is informal evaluation of the consultants by their colleagues in the consultation class and by their consultees in the schools.

Regarding evaluation by the course instructor and graduate assistant, consultants are informed that their course grade will be comprised of various components of their work, and that they will *not* be graded on growth in their clients or consultees. They are told this because some settings are much more difficult to work in, as is illustrated in the case example presented here. Some field supervisors place more restraints on consultants than others. Some consultants are willing to tackle bigger issues or more resistant consultees, and growth in others in these situations may be slower or more difficult to assess. These are just three of the reasons why it is important that consultants be given this message.

Consultants are told that they will be graded on the following: class participation, demonstrated familiarity with course readings, quality of oral and written presentations, some acceptable level of work in the field placement, and openness to and work in supervision. They are evaluated according to how they conceptualize and reflect on their work, rather than the actual outcome of their work. This approach allows the consultants to freely engage in the process of learning about consultation, without becoming discouraged by the daunting nature of working in real-world settings without yet having mastered the skills necessary to fully serve these settings. As has been noted elsewhere, fieldwork experience can enable consultation trainees to develop the judgmental competencies needed to deal with the consultees they will encounter in their roles (Brown, 1993).

The case example described here illustrates this point. Had the consultant been expected to bring about a predetermined level of change, she would have been set up to fail. By focusing on consultation as a process, she and the other consultants in the class were able to engage in valuable learning that enabled them to broaden and deepen their experience base, as well as their understanding of the complexities of consultation. Although the process may have been difficult and frustrating at times, the consultant, through first-hand experience, recognized that to bring about change is often not an easy task. In this case, the consultant gained a more thorough awareness of how to approach issues and problems than she might have had everything run smoothly.

The course instructor and graduate assistant together assign grades and the course instructor is ultimately responsible for the grades. In determining the grade, the evaluation by the consultants and the field supervisor are considered. Later in the course the consultants are told that, in addition to the faculty assessing their performance, the consultant must as well. They are asked to think about how they operationalize success as a consultant. Often they will cite changes in attitudes or behavior in the clients or consultees or themselves. They will be reminded that their year of consultation was one of entry. They are told that the instructor thinks they were successful if they feel they would consult more wisely next time. They are reminded about what they were like at the beginning of the year: anxious and with little knowledge of consultation theory or practice. They speak to their disappointment in what they accomplished over the year. They are instructed about the *"three consultation Rs,"* which are resources, recognition, and role.

Resources involve, for example, number of days and length of time they are in the placement. They need to have a realistic time perspective as to what can be accomplished given limited time in the setting. *Recognition* involves knowing oneself and knowing one's environment. Attaining this wisdom takes time. *Role* involves their marginal status. While they work as consultants, they are students and they do not receive payment. Given their student status and lack of payment for consultation, staff commitment will be less.

They are told that their expectations should be small given these three Rs and that if they expect success they are positioning themselves for failure. They are told that success is impossible, not because they are inadequate, but because of the *"three consultation Rs."* Their resources and role have been limited, and recognition takes time. Consultants are encouraged to think about *partial success*. Reasonable goals are identified. Some include: to have a better sense of consultation and specifically what it means, and to have knowledge about how to work consultatively.

The professor then relates her perspective, which is that she feels successful as an instructor if she knows that *they* have learned. She asks what they have learned about the following: establishing contracts and renegotiating contracts, entry, gaining credibility, helping and understanding and appreciating the indirect service model, a theory of schools, how things change, working with others, and establishing priorities and time perspective. They are also encouraged to think about: how things change, their values and how they influence they way the work, their personal style, being external and internal to a system, diagnosis, evaluation, group process, and so on.

On the first day of class the consultants write their definitions of consultation. They are asked to write them on the last day as well. The early definitions are returned and compared with their end-of-year understanding. Students confront their learning. These and similar discussions and exercises help consultants to assess their success in a more realistic manner.

While the field supervisor is encouraged to complete an evaluation form with the consultant and these forms are made available to the course instructor, this information does not determine course grade. However, it is considered. When there are great discrepancies in opinion, efforts are made to understand why. The student consultants will engage in these deliberations. Informal evaluation of the student consultants by their colleagues in the consultation class or by their consultees in the school are not considered in the evaluation process. Regarding the latter, the reason is that if the student consultant was truly helpful to a consultee, the consultee will think changes were a function of his/her own activity rather than the consultants.

IMPLICATIONS FOR TRAINING AND RESEARCH

In summary, in 1983, Alpert and Meyers indicated that there had been relatively little attention to consultation training in the literature. The situation has not changed much in the last 20 years. Ten years later, Brown (1993) pointed to the lack of attention paid to developing consultation skills in counselor education programs. Hellkamp et al. (1998) made another call for convening a national conference on educational standards in consulting psychology. In 2002, the need for such a conference continues to be great.

With respect to the three questions discussed here, the following recommendations for training may be considered. Training of consultants should include didactic, practicum, and fieldwork experiences to provide trainees with breadth and depth of specialized knowledge. Such tripartite training serves as an example of how to integrate theory and practice. Students should be provided with opportunities to observe effective consultation practice, ideally through their fieldwork settings. If this is not possible, the tripartite training model can allow for such opportunities through one of the other training components. In addition, students will benefit from multiple sources of supervision as they develop their consulting skills.

Research also needs to be done to determine how other programs conceptualize these issues. One next step would be to attempt to compare different training models in an effort to learn about effective training. Specifically, future research may address issues of placement selection, fieldwork selection, and evaluation of the work and development of consultants. For example, empirical research is needed to determine how best to match consultants with placements from the perspective of both. This research may be modeled after the research grounded in ecological perspectives, focusing on matching students with particular classroom environments (i.e., Trickett, 1997). With respect to schools, Moos and Trickett (1979) examined how school classrooms differ in various types of schools, as well as the relations between different variables within the ecological environment and classroom climate. Future research may also be modeled after existing research on matching students' learning styles and needs with teachers' teaching techniques (Corno & Snow, 1986). By adapting such research to the training of consultants, researchers may be able to systematically address issues that arise in consultation training. Some questions that may be asked are: How are students most appropriately placed in settings, in a way that fits the needs of both students and settings? Are trainees best suited to certain placements according to their degree goals (MA/MS, Psy.D., or Ph.D.)? What are the advantages and disadvantages to placing students in settings that are not receptive to consultation as compared to those in which consultation is easier to do?

In summary, the intent of this article is to put three questions that arise before students enter the consultation course into currency. It is hoped it will stimulate more discussion about these as well as other questions related to consultation training. It is time to begin to focus on consultation training.

ACKNOWLEDGMENT

This article is an edited and updated version of a paper presented as part of a symposium, "Teaching Consultation for Over Eighty Years—Collectively, That Is," at the Annual Convention of the American Psychological Association Convention, August 7, 2000, Washington, DC, J.L. Alpert, Chair.

REFERENCES

Adams, R. S., & Weinick, H. N. (1966). Consultation: An inservice training program for the school. *Journal of the American Academy of Child Psychiatry, 5,* 479–489.

Alessi, G. J., Lascurettes-Alessi, K. J., & Leys, W. L. (1981). Internships in school psychology: Supervision issues. *School Psychology Review, 10,* 461–469.

Alpert, J. L., Feit, D., & Grant, C. (1983). Supervisory Models. In J. L. Alpert & J. Meyers (Eds.), *Training in consultation: Perspectives from mental health, behavioral and organizational consultation* (pp. 203–212). Springfield, IL:Thomas.

Alpert, J. L., Ludwig, L., & Weiner, L. (1979). Selection of consultees in school mental health consultation. *Journal of School Psychology, 17,* 59–66.

Alpert, J. L., & Meyers, J. (Eds.). (1983). *Training in consultation: Perspectives from mental health, behavioral and organizational consultation.* Springfield, IL:Thomas.

Alpert, J. L., & Paulson, A. (1990). Graduate-level education and training in child sexual abuse. *Professional Psychology: Research and Practice, 21,* 366–371.

Alpert, J. L., Silverstein, J. M., & Haynes, R. (1980). Utilization of groups in training for school consultation. *Journal of School Psychology, 18,* 240–246.

Alpert, J. L., Weiner, L., & Ludwig, L. (1979). Evaluation of outcome in school consultation. *Journal of School Psychology, 17,* 69–84.

Atella, M. D., & Figgatt, J. E. (1998). Practicums in consulting psychology: Working with doctoral clinical programs. *Consulting Psychology Journal: Practice and Research, 50,* 218–227.

Berlin, I. N. (2001). A retrospective view of school mental health consultation. *Child and Adolescent Psychiatric Clinics of North America, 10,* 25–31.

Brown, D. (1993). Training consultants: A call to action. *Journal of Counseling and Development, 72,* 139–143.

Canter, S., & Feder, B. (1968). Psychological consultation in Head Start programs. *American Psychologist, 23,* 590–592.

Caplan, G. (1970). *The theory and practice of mental health consultation.* New York: Basic Books.

Caplan, G., & Caplan, R. B. (1993). *Mental health consultation and collaboration.* San Francisco: Jossey-Bass.

Corno, L., & Snow, R. E. (1986). Adapting teaching to individual differences among learners. In M. C. Wittrock (Ed.), *Handbook of research on teaching* (3rd ed., pp. 605–629). New York: MacMillian.

Crespi, T. D., & Lopez, P. G. (1998). Practicum and internship supervision in the schools: Standards and considerations for school psychology supervisors. *Clinical Supervisor, 17,* 113–126.

Curtis, M. J., & Zins, J. E. (1988). Effects of training in consultation and instructor feedback on acquisition of consultation skills. *Journal of School Psychology, 26,* 185–190.

Ehly, S. W., Dustin, D., Bratton, B., Ritter, K. Y., Keller, J. W., Piotrowski, C., et al. (1987). Describing graduate placements. In M. E. Ware & R. J. Millard (Eds.), *Handbook on student development: Advising, career development, and field placement* (pp. 244–251). Hillsdale, NJ: Lawrence Erlbaum Associates, Inc.

Fagan, T. K., & Wise, P. S. (1994). *School psychology: Past, present, and future.* White Plains, NY: Longman.

Gallessich, J., Long, K. M., & Jennings, S. (1986). Training of mental health consultants. In F. V. Mannino & E. J. Trickett (Eds.), *Handbook of mental health consultation* (pp. 279–317). Rockville, MD: National Institute of Mental Health.

Gatmon, D., Jackson, D., Koshkarian, L., Martos-Perry, N., Molina, A., Patel, N., et al. (2001). Exploring ethnic, gender, and sexual orientation variables in supervision: Do they really matter? *Journal of Multicultural Counseling and Development, 29*(2), 102–113.

Goode, E. (2001, August 1). Study says 20% of girls reported abuse by a date. *The New York Times,* p. A10.

Greenberg, H. A., Bettelheim, B., Perkins, G. L., Wright, B., Riley, M. J., & Adland, M. (1958). Psychiatric consultation in residential treatment: Workshop, 1957. *American Journal of Orthopsychiatry, 28,* 256–290.

Harper, D. J., & Spellman, D. (1994). Consultation to a professional network: Reflections of a would-be consultant. *Journal of Family Therapy, 16,* 383–399.

Hellkamp, D. T., Zins, J. E., Ferguson, K., & Hodge, M. (1998). Training practices in consultation: A national survey of clinical, counseling, industrial/organizational, and school psychology faculty. *Consulting Psychology Journal: Practice and Research, 50,* 228–236.

Hitchcock, J., & Mooney, W. E. (1969). Mental health consultation: A psychoanalytic formulation. *Archives of General Psychiatry, 21,* 353–358.

Kratochwill, T. R., & Bergan, J. R. (1978). Training school psychologists: Some perspectives on a competency-based behavioral consultation model. *Professional Psychology: Research and Practice, 9,* 71–82.

Kratochwill, T. R., Sheridan, S. M., Carrington-Rotto, P., & Salmon, D. (1992). Preparation of school psychologists in behavioral consultation service delivery. In T. R. Kratochwill & S. N. Elliott (Eds.), *Advances in school psychology* (Vol. 8, pp. 115–152). Hillsdale, NJ: Lawrence Erlbaum Associates, Inc.

Kratochwill, T. R., & Van Someren, K. R. (1984). Training behavioral consultants: Issues and directions. *Behavior Therapist, 7,* 19–22.

Libo, L. M. (1966). Multiple functions for psychologists in community consultation. *American Psychologist, 21,* 530–534.

Lifschutz, J. E., Stewart, T. B., & Harrison, A. M. (1958). Psychiatric consultation in the public assistance agency. *Social Casework, 39,* 3–9.

Loomis, S. D. (1966). Psychiatric consultation in a delinquent population. *American Journal of Psychiatry, 123,* 66–70.

Maddux, J. F. (1953). Psychiatric consultation in a rural setting. *American Journal of Orthopsychiatry, 23,* 775–784.

Mariner, A. S., Brandt, E., Stone, E. C., & Mirmow, E. L. (1961). Group psychiatric consultation with public school personnel: A two-year study. *Personnel and Guidance Journal, 40,* 254–258.

Meyers, J. (1984). Training in consultation. *American Journal of Community Psychology, 12,* 233–239.

Meyers, J., Wurtz, R., & Flanagan, D. (1981). A national survey investigating consultation training occurring in school psychology programs. *Psychology in the Schools, 18*(3), 297–302.

Millar, T. P. (1966). Psychiatric consultation with classroom teachers. *Journal of the American Academy of Child Psychiatry, 5*(1), 134–144.

Moos, R. H., & Trickett, E. J. (1979). Determinants of classroom environments. In R. H. Moos (Ed.), *Evaluating educational environments* (pp. 159–182). San Francisco: Jossey-Bass.

Newman, R. G. (1967). *Psychological consultation in the schools: A catalyst for learning.* New York: Basic Books.

Peebles, M. J., & O'Malley, F. (1978). Problems in mental health consultation facing the professional in training. *Journal of Clinical Child Psychology, 7*(1), 68–70.

Pinkerton, R., & Temple, R. D. (2000). Mental health consultation and psychology internship training. *Professional Psychology: Research and Practice, 31,* 315–320.

Putney, M. W., Worthington, E. L., & McCullough, M. E. (1992). Effects of supervisor and supervisee theoretical orientation and supervisor-supervisee matching on interns' perceptions of supervision. *Journal of Counseling Psychology, 39,* 258–265.

Robiner, W. N., Saltzman, S. R., Hoberman, H. M., Semrud-Clikeman, M., & Schirvar, J. A. (1998). *Clinical Supervisor, 16*(2), 49–72.

Romans, J. S. C., Boswell, D. L., Carlozzi, A. F., & Ferguson, D. B. (1995). Training and supervision practices in clinical, counseling, and school psychology programs. *Professional Psychology: Research and Practice, 26*(4), 407–412.

Ross, R. P., & Goh, D. S. (1993). Participating in supervision in school psychology: A national survey of practices and training. *School Psychology Review, 22*(1), 63–80.

Ryan, D. J., Lombardi, K., Liederman, B., & Zelinger, F. (1980). The intensive multisupervisory internship in school psychology. *Psychology in the Schools, 17*(2), 216–221.

Sarason, S. B. (1966). *Psychology in community settings.* New York: Wiley.

Shearer, M. (1968). The principal is often overlooked. *Community Mental Health Journal, 4*(1), 47–52.

Sheridan, S. M. (1992). Consultant and client outcomes of competency-based behavioral consultation training. *School Psychology Quarterly, 7,* 245–270.

Sheridan, S. M. (1997). Conceptual and empirical bases of conjoint behavioral consultation. *School Psychology Quarterly, 12,* 119–133.

Sheridan, S. M., Salmon, D., Kratochwill, T. R., Carrington-Rotto, P. J. (1992). A conceptual model for the expansion of behavioral consultation training. *Journal of Educational and Psychological Consultation, 3,* 193–218.

Sterling-Turner, H. E., Watson, T. S., Wildmon, M., Watkins, C., & Little, E. (2001). Investigating the relationship between training type and treatment integrity. *School Psychology Quarterly, 16,* 56–67.

Stoltenberg, C. D. (1993). Supervising consultants in training: An application of a model of supervision. *Journal of Counseling and Development, 72,* 131–138.

Sussman, R. B., & Zimberg, S. (1967). Psychiatric consultation with public schools in an underprivileged neighborhood. *American Journal of Orthopsychiatry, 37,* 340–341.

Toenes, B. D., Lytle, C. E., Wagner, N. N., & Wimberger, H. C. (1968). The diagnostic consultation and rural community mental health programs. *Community Mental Health Journal, 4,* 157–163.

Trickett, E. J. (1997). Developing an ecological mind-set on school-community collaboration. In J. L. Swartz & W. E. Martin (Eds.), *Applied ecological psychology for schools within communities* (pp. 139–166). Mahwah, NJ: Lawrence Erlbaum Associates, Inc.

Van Velsor, P. R., & Cox, D. L. (2000). Use of the collaborative drawing technique in school counseling practicum: An illustration of family systems. *Counselor Education and Supervision, 40,* 141–152.

Walsh, W. M., & Williams, G. R. (1997). *Schools and family therapy: Using systems theory and family therapy in the resolution of school problems.* Springfield, IL: Thomas.

Ware, M. E., & Millard, R. J. (Eds.). (1987). *Handbook on student development: Advising, career development, and field placement.* Hillsdale, NJ: Lawrence Erlbaum Associates, Inc.

Westman, J. C. (1968). Psychiatric contributions to school health programs. *Hospital and Community Psychiatry, 19*(8), 258–260.

Williams, M. E. (1967). Help for the teacher of disturbed children in the public school: The use of consultation for problem solving and personal growth. *Exceptional Children, 34*(2), 87–91.

Zins, J. E. (1989). Building applied experiences into a consultation training program. *Consultation: An International Journal, 8,* 191–201.

Zins, J. E., & Murphy, J. J. (1996). Consultation with professional peers: A national survey of the practices of school psychologists. *Journal of Educational and Psychological Consultation, 7,* 61-70.

Judith L. Alpert is Professor of Applied Psychology at New York University. Her research interests include: child sexual abuse, date and acquaintance violence, school violence, and prevention.

Shilpa Taufique, M.A. is a doctoral candidate at New York University. Her research interests include consultation, relation between culture and child abuse, school violence, and prevention.

JOURNAL OF EDUCATIONAL AND PSYCHOLOGICAL CONSULTATION, 13(1&2), 35–54

A 30 Year Perspective On Best Practices for Consultation Training

Joel Meyers

Georgia State University

This article uses the author's 30 years of teaching consultation as a basis for developing suggestions for those providing training in this field. The article addresses questions about what the content of training should be, how consultation training can link theory to practice and how to respond to persistent challenges to training (e.g., freedom versus constraint, multicultural consultation, and when consultation training should be offered within a preservice curriculum for developing school-based consultants). The training suggestions derive from a model of consultation and consultation training that is based in constructivism and seeks to enhance feelings of empowerment and long term implementation of consultation on the part of the trainee. The article proposes a practitioner–researcher model in which practicing consultants view themselves as researchers who collect data and share information about their practice with other school-based consultants. These shared practices are used to inform the knowledge base and are used as a basis for contributing to the scholarly literature. Finally, this article proposes directions for researching the process and outcome of consultation training that cut across all of the issues raised in this article.

The graduate training that I received at New York University (1966–1967) and the University of Texas–Austin (1967–1970) introduced me to two ideas that have had substantial effects on my career: (1) that it might be possible to prevent psychopathology by working with *all* children in school; and (2) that consultation can be used by school psychologists and other educators to help teachers develop school-based interventions to promote a

---

Correspondence should be addressed to Joel Meyers, Department of Counseling and Psychological Services, Georgia State University, Atlanta, GA 30303–3083. E-mail: jpmeyers@gsu.edu

range of preventive goals. The potential of these two ideas convinced me that school-based practice offers the most productive way to apply psychological principles to help children. In this context, I was particularly excited because schools provide an opportunity to reach all children who might need help regardless of their circumstances.

Since that time, I have practiced school-based consultation, conducted applied research about this topic, and taught consultation to graduate students in school psychology for a 30-year period as a member of the faculties at Temple University, the University at Albany (SUNY), Georgia State University, and as an adjunct faculty member at Alfred University, the University of Minnesota, and the University of Puerto Rico. As a result, I have developed a model of mental health consultation that uses a combination of psychodynamic, cognitive–behavioral and ecological principles within a constructivist framework that seeks to empower the consultee (Henning-Stout, 1994; Ingraham, 2000; Meyers, 1995; 1998; Rappaport, 1981; Truscott, Cosgrove, Meyers, & Eidle-Barkman, 2000). This model emphasizes indirect service to the child as well as methods that prevent the development of learning and adjustment problems in children.

The purpose of this article is to share some of the important things that I have learned about training school-based consultants by raising fundamental questions, as well as suggesting future directions. The article addresses questions about the content of training, how consultation training can link theory to practice, and how to respond to persistent challenges about training (e.g., freedom versus constraint, multicultural consultation, and when consultation training should be offered within preservice curricula for school-based practitioners). In addition, the article proposes directions for researching the process and outcome of consultation training.

WHAT SHOULD BE THE CONTENT OF COURSEWORK IN SCHOOL-BASED CONSULTATION?

It is not possible to do justice to this question in the confines of one brief article on issues in training. This would require consideration of all essential elements of consultation research and practice (i.e., the content of consultation training), while simultaneously considering a range of strategies for providing consultation training. There are numerous excellent sources related to school-based consultation that provide detailed information about the practice of consultation that might be the focus of training (e.g., Bergan & Kratochwill, 1990; Brown, Pryswansky & Schulte, 1995; Caplan &

Caplan, 1993; Conoley & Conoley, 1992; Erchul & Martens, 1997; Gutkin & Curtis, 1999; Marks, 1995; Meyers, Parsons & Martin, 1979; Parsons & Meyers, 1984; Rosenfield, 1987). In addition to these references, some of my recent ideas about school-based consultation were discussed in a recent journal article (Meyers, 1995). I teach the model of mental health consultation that was delineated in the prior section of this article. In addition, I exposed students to a range of theoretical perspectives including mental health (Caplan & Caplan, 1993), behavioral (Bergan & Kratochwill, 1990), and ecobehavioral consultation (Gutkin & Curtis, 1999). The article delineating my approach to consultation, along with the combination of theoretical perspectives that are incorporated into my model, provide the basis for the syllabus[1] that I use when teaching consultation.

Over the years, I have developed two consultation courses. The first consultation course is focused on child-centered and consultee-centered consultation and includes a practicum that usually focuses on a child-centered case. In this course students spend at least 1 day per week working on their consultation case. Students are supervised by an on-site practicum supervisor who supervises all components of their school practicum. Additional supervision regarding the consultation case is provided by the instructor during class time on a weekly basis and outside of class as needed. The second course follows the first and comes later in the training program. It is focused on organizational consultation and the prevention of learning and adjustment problems. This article focuses primarily on the first course. Some of the topics from the consultation syllabus are highlighted briefly in the following section because they may be particularly important for novice consultants to learn early in training.

Levels of Consultation and an Emphasis on Indirect Services

One key goal of consultation training is to help trainees learn about the different types of consultation that can be offered such as child-centered, consultee-centered (i.e., teacher/classroom-centered), and system-centered consultation (e.g., see Caplan & Caplan, 1993; Gutkin & Curtis, 1999; Marks, 1995; Meyers, 1995). These can be conceptualized as levels of consultation that vary in the degree to which services are provided directly to children and the most indirect services are characterized by their potential

---

[1]Copies of the syllabus for the courses that I teach on consultation can be obtained by contacting Joel Meyers at Georgia State University (jpmeyers@gsu.edu).

to reach the maximum number of children. This encourages consultants to learn strategies that emphasize prevention by using the most indirect services (i.e., system-wide, class-wide, or teacher-centered problems), rather than emphasizing the more direct services such as child-centered consultation that focuses on problems of the individual student. This focus implies that consultant trainees must learn strategies for organizational consultation as well as strategies that facilitate solutions to individual children's difficulties.

Although consultee-centered and system-centered consultation may be viewed as more indirect services than child-centered consultation, all types of consultation are indirect approaches to delivering services to children. The indirect nature of consultation means that the consultant must rely on someone else (e.g., the consultee) to take responsibility for implementing interventions to help children, and this is important to consider when training consultants (Gutkin & Conoley, 1990). Gallessich (1983) reinforced this point by indicating that many of those receiving training in consultation have come into the fields of psychology and education because of their desire to help needy children and their prior experiencing directly helping such children. An important goal of consultation training is to help trainees overcome preexisting motivations for helping individual children directly, by developing a preventive orientation that motivates consultants in training to help larger numbers of children indirectly by assisting caregivers (i.e., consultees) who will in turn help the needy children under their care (see Gallessich, 1983; Meyers, Brent, Faherty, & Modafferi, 1993).

Consultation and Prevention

School-based consultation can be used to develop and implement preventive strategies in schools. Prevention can be conceptualized as including four areas (Meyers & Nastasi, 1999): primary prevention (targeted to the entire population), risk reduction (preventive strategies targeted to groups of the population that are known to have been placed at risk), early intervention (preventive strategies targeted to those showing early signs of a disorder) and treatment (intervention targeted to those experiencing a disorder). Prior literature on school-based consultation has not emphasized sufficiently that consultation can be used to help schools implement each of the four types of prevention. Unfortunately, consultants most often pursue goals associated with "treatment" and to a lesser extent "early intervention." As a result, there are lost opportunities to use consultation to facilitate "primary prevention," "risk reduction" and even "early intervention" because many consultants remain unaware that these are realistic goals of consultation (e.g., see Meyers & Nastasi, 1999). Training can help to make the critical connections between consultation and prevention early in the student's career.

For example, consultee-centered consultation focuses on the teacher, the classroom, and generally has implications to improve the learning or adjustment of a range of students in the classroom, or both, rather than being limited to a single problem student. This creates potential for primary prevention or risk reduction strategies because of the focus on the environment (i.e., classroom or teacher or both) and because a range of students can benefit from consultation. Similarly, organizational consultation focuses on the school (or school district) as a system. This approach has implications for a range of educators in the system and for a wide range of students in addition to single students who might be referred. As a result, this creates similar, and sometimes broader, opportunities for primary prevention and risk reduction. In this context, consultants can help a maximum number of students by maintaining a focus on universal interventions (e.g., social skills and life skills curricula), interventions for groups of children who have been placed at risk (e.g., children who have been exposed to drug abuse, community violence, and so forth), screening strategies to pick out children who need "early intervention" services, young children (e.g., pre-Kindergarten and grades K–3), and interventions for children exposed to significant life transitions (e.g., school entry, entrance to middle school and high school, students moving to a new community, children of divorce, children who have lost a caretaker to illness or death, and so forth) (see Meyers & Nastasi, 1999).

Problem Solving Stages

Training in consultation must emphasize problem solving stages and these have numerous descriptions in the consultation literature (e.g., see Gutkin & Curtis, 1999). I alert students to the range of stages presented in the literature and underscore the following stages: contract negotiation and problem identification, data collection and problem analysis, intervention development, intervention implementation, and evaluation. Although it is not necessarily important which ones are used, there is substantial evidence that systematic use of problem solving stages contributes to effective consultation and that ineffective consultants often skip important steps such as contract negotiation, problem identification and data collection (e.g., Bergan & Tombari, 1978; Flugum & Reschly, 1994; Meyers, Valentino, Meyers, Boretti, & Brent, 1996).

It may be necessary to use problem solving stages, but this is not always easy to carry out in practice. Trainees need to learn effective strategies that help school personnel develop the patience needed to use problem solving stages. I encourage consultant trainees to involve consultees actively in collecting and analyzing data. This is done by helping the teacher develop data collection strategies that are practical for them to implement and have high acceptability to the teacher. In this context, it can be useful to suggest that teachers record anecdotal notes at the end of each day for a short period of time, use frequency count recording on relatively infrequent behaviors, or use time sampling methods where the teachers' observations are focused for short practical time periods. Also, it can be effective to have the consultant develop an observation recording form to facilitate the teacher's observation efforts or to help the teacher develop a self-observation system that the child can implement. In addition, I encourage consultant trainees to involve teachers in the problem solving stages by having them develop interventions collaboratively with the teacher. When this does not occur easily because a teacher is reluctant to participate, I encourage the use of strategies such as having the consultant and teacher engage in a brainstorming process where they alternate making suggestions of potential interventions. Furthermore, I encourage consultant trainees to use a problem solving sheet that includes the consultation stages.[2] In this way both consultant and consultee work together to keep a record of their efforts to engage systematically in each of the problem solving stages.

Interpersonal Process Skills

Training in consultation should help trainees develop expertise in the interpersonal process skills needed to ensure effective consultation. The consultation literature indicates a range of such variables that can be used by consultants to facilitate effective consultation and these include strategies that maintain a collaborative interchange between colleagues who have equal status in terms of power, freedom of the consultee to accept or reject recommendations, emphasis on the consultee's contributions to consultation outcome, and effective communication strategies (e.g., see Bergan &

---

[2] An example of a consultation problem solving sheet that incorporates a written record of the stages used in consultation can be obtained by contacting Joel Meyers at Georgia State University (jpmeyers@gsu.edu).

Kratochwill, 1990; Caplan & Caplan, 1993; Erchul, 1999; Gutkin, 1997; Gutkin, 1999; Gutkin & Curtis, 1999; Meyers, 1995).

Group and Individual Consultation

Twenty years ago Chris Keys (1983) suggested that it an important challenge in consultation training was the decision about whether to focus on group or individual consultation. The increased attention to prereferral intervention teams as a method of implementing consultation makes this point even more important today, and requires that consultation training include some attention to group consultation. Much of the prior research literature on school-based consultation concerns a dyadic relationship between one consultant and one teacher. Prereferral intervention teams provide a group of consultants (often a multidisciplinary team) that provides consultative assistance to a referring teacher. Evidence is emerging that prereferral intervention teams can be effective in helping teachers to solve and prevent problems (e.g., see Eidle, Truscott, Meyers, & Boyd, 1998; Meyers et al., 1996; Rosenfield & Gravois, 1996). There is also an emerging data base suggesting that consultation provided by a group of consultants can present unique issues concerning group process and team decision making (e.g., when one team member dominates, decisions are made without consensus of team members, or teachers feel threatened by the consultation team, or both; Gutkin & Nemeth, 1997; Meyers et al., 1996).

Consultation can also be offered to a group of consultees. Although there has been less research about this type of group consultation, there is some empirical support for this approach and this raises unique issues concerning group process (e.g., see Babinski & Rogers, 1998; Brown, Wyne, Blackburn & Powell, 1979; Caplan & Caplan, 1993; Cohen & Osterweil, 1986; Dinkmeyer & Carlson, 1973). Training needs to focus on both approaches to "group consultation" as well as providing solid training on effective strategies for dyadic consultation (see Caplan & Caplan, 1993; Cohern & Osterweill, 1986; Gutkin & Curtis, 1999; Gutkin & Nemeth, 1997; Meyers et al., 1996).

HOW CAN WE LINK THEORY AND PRACTICE?

Like many applied components of the fields of education and psychology, school based consultation is a training topic that is ideally suited for linking both theory and research with practice. Theoretical models underlying consultation directly influence the behavior of practitioners. For example, behavioral, cognitive, constructivist, ecological, and psychodynamic theories require different consultation procedures under certain circumstances and it is important to help trainees develop clarity about these issues. Also, theoretical ideas about prevention, interpersonal process, problem solving stages, and the levels of indirect service in consultation have significant implications for consultants' choices in practice. Therefore, training must be provided in ways that make these connections.

Applied training activities like role playing, modeling and practicum can be important ways to underscore the links between theory or research and practice. These kinds of training activities must be implemented in ways that pay careful and systematic attention to underlying theory. For example, when role playing, modeling or discussing a consultation case from practicum, a critical role of trainers is to draw out the implications for existing theory *and* research.

Two principles of consultation training are particularly applicable for consultation trainers seeking to make the link between theory or research and practice. One principle is to make applied training activities as real as possible. I strongly prefer practicum-based activities to strengthen learning, as opposed to role plays. As a result, students in my initial consultation class begin their school-based consultation practicum experience early in the semester. They tape record their consultation so that live case examples can be brought to class to enrich learning for all class members.

When I determine that it is important to use "role plays" in class (i.e., prior to students engaging in their first consultation interview), I have the students consult with each other about a real problem (often a problem related to their colleague's consultation case from the practicum), rather than making up a problem and playing roles associated with this problem. In addition, when I model consultation strategies, I consult with a teacher or a class member about a real problem, rather than making up a problem to discuss. All of these approaches to classroom demonstration by the instructor or by class members are structured so that some class members serve as observers who later provide feedback to stimulate class discussion. There is a need for future research to provide data addressing the effectiveness of these approaches, as well as the conditions that influence their efficacy.

The second important training principle that might be considered is to have students make connections between theory or research and practice through structured discussions about cases in the context of the didactic material being covered. I try not to tell students what these connections are, but first, encourage them to think about and discuss potential connections between theory or research, or both, and consultation practice. I use the discussion format to insert my own views of these connections, but I believe that the most sustained learning will occur based on those connections that students discover. This perspective and the related strategies derive from the constructivist framework that supports the consultation courses that I teach.

At the 1980 conference on consultation training, it was suggested that one important challenge to consultation training is the tension between scientific and practitioner approaches, because of the expectation that focusing on one of these topics would take away from the other (Keys, 1983). Although I understand the basis for this thinking, I believe that this potential problem can be overcome by integrating research in practice. For example, implementing problem solving stages in consultation requires the use of research skills to collect data in defining the problem and determining the efficacy of consultation interventions. Moreover, the problem solving stages used in consultation overlap substantially with problem solving stages used in approaches to program evaluation and collaborative action research (e.g., see LeCompte & Schensul, 1999; Meyers & Nastasi, 1999; i.e., contract negotiation, problem identification, data collection and data analysis, intervention development, and evaluation). These approaches include the use of qualitative methods and they need to receive more attention from educators and psychologists.

The linkages of practice with the underlying science and theory of consultation can be strengthened by using the "practitioner researcher" model (referred to elsewhere as the "school psychologist as researcher;" Meyers, 1998). This perspective is based on the "teacher researcher" model that has influenced thinking about teaching and training teachers (Cochran-Smith & Lytle, 1993, 2000). This model suggests that practicing school-based consultants should research their own practice in an effort to strengthen their performance while contributing to the knowledge base about consultation. Implementing this model requires that students receive training regarding "practitioner–research."

One argument for applying this model to consultation is the need for more research on the process and outcome of consultation (e.g., Meyers, 1995, 1998). If school based consultants engaged in research as a routine component of their practice, this could add needed information to the developing knowledge base in this area. The existing body of research on consultation has been dominated by academic researchers rather than practicing consultants, and this has resulted in research that is based on questions and research designs that are of interest to the academic community, but may not be grounded by the perspectives of practitioners who use consultation (Cochran-Smith & Lytle, 1993, 2000; Meyers, 1998; Meyers & Nastasi, 1999). Consultants using the practitioner researcher model should routinely use practical research strategies (including qualitative or quantitative methods or both) to evaluate and improve their own practice and then disseminate information learned from this applied research. This is a recent addition to my own thinking about consultation that is influencing my efforts to teach consultation.

Although the practitioner–researcher model proposed here may be a compelling approach to link theory and practice that has the potential to strengthen the efficacy of services provided by school-based practitioners, it presents some important challenges in training. How can we train students to be practitioner–researchers given the high probability that they may be quickly acculturated to the practitioner culture during internship and practicum (e.g., consultation field supervisors may not be familiar with the practitioner–researcher)? This is a significant problem for those training programs that include school-based practicum and internship experiences.

There are no simple answers, however, developing a cadre of school professionals who understand this approach would provide students with support for using practitioner–researcher strategies in practica and internships. This cadre of school professionals should receive training in the practitioner–researcher model and should be offered support by the university for their own efforts at implementation so that they can serve as models for students learning this approach. University faculty can also be constructive models if they are visible school-based service providers who are explicit in their use of the practitioner–researcher model. Finally, ongoing support groups can be developed for school-based professionals implementing the practitioner-researcher model and this can be done in interaction with the university (e.g., see Cochran-Smith & Lytle, 1993, for a description of an enduring teacher–research group—the Philadelphia Writing Project).

THE NEED FOR RESEARCH ON
CONSULTATION TRAINING

One recent survey of practicing school psychologists (Costenbader, Swartz, & Petrix, 1992) indicated that only 61% of respondents reported receiving at least one full semester of training in consultation and 53% of respondents did not rate training as adequate (i.e., 53%). Furthermore, few respondents indicated that they use the model that was the focus of their training (i.e., 53% were trained in behavioral consultation, but only 38% report using this model; 32% trained in mental health consultation, but only 9% report using this model; and 26% reported that they use no model at all). Multiple interpretations of these data are possible. Data such as these have led some to question the efficacy of consultation training because training may be too brief to result in the mastery needed for application in practice (Erchul & Martens, 1997). On the other hand, the data suggesting that trainees use models that differ from the model that was the focus of their training may indicate that these psychologists have learned flexible approaches that allow them to match strategies to the needs of their setting. There is a need for additional research that would help to determine the underlying meaning for such survey data, and in this context, it is underscored that there has been very little research examining consultation training and its impact.

Will Consultation Trainers Dare to Research Their Own Practice?

Alpert's (1983) presidential address to the Division of School Psychology (16) of the American Psychological Association made the point that university based educators and psychologists readily recommend that preventive interventions be implemented and evaluated in K–12 schools, but rarely heed their own suggestions by applying these approaches to their own universities. Similarly, academics recommend consultation as a method of service delivery, they conduct research about consultation, but they rarely research the efficacy of their efforts to provide training in consultation. Thus, I would argue that university faculty with expertise in consultation need to apply these strategies to solve problems in their universities, research the effectiveness of such change efforts as well as researching the efficacy of the consultation training that they provide.

If student-centered, teacher-centered, and system-centered approaches to consultation can help schools, they should surely be able to help universities. For example, if teacher problems concerning knowledge, skill, and objectivity can affect performance in public school settings, surely these issues can affect performance in universities. Similarly, if system-centered issues can affect performance in public schools, surely these issues can affect learning in universities.

Consultation practice, consultation training and our related knowledge base would be likely to improve substantially if there were systematic efforts to apply consultation in universities, to research the efficacy of this consultation and to research the processes and outcomes of consultation training. In this context, note that there have been some beginning efforts to offer consultation in university settings (e.g., see Bardon, 1982; Kressel, Bailey, & Forman, 1999) and there have been some efforts of university faculty to research the efficacy of the consultation training that they offer (e.g., Hasbrouck, Parker, & Tindal, 1999).

In addition to contributing useful information, research on university practices such as consultation and consultation training would model for trainees that it can be realistic to apply consultation and to research practice in our own settings. Until academics take this challenge seriously, they cannot expect to develop reflective practitioners who research and improve their own consultation practice in the schools that employ them.

OTHER PERSISTENT CHALLENGES IN CONSULTATION TRAINING

Freedom Versus Constraint

In his presentation at the conference on consultation training in 1980, Chris Keys (1983) suggested that a critical issue in consultation training is to determine the degree to which freedom should be given to trainees during training. This continues to be an important consideration in consultation training and I suspect (though I don't have a data base to support this claim) that currently those providing training in consultation may give too much weight to constraint at the expense of freedom. I say this because we know a great deal more about how to conduct consultation at this time than we did 30 years ago when consultation training was in its infancy, and I suspect that this knowledge may make consultation trainers emphasize their "right way" to provide consultation.

One example of this dilemma derives from my own experience learning consultation. One of the most important strengths of the consultation training that I received was the freedom to develop my own ideas about consultation and to experiment with strategies for implementing these ideas. As a result, I internalized what was learned and have tried to modify my approaches over time based on experience and research. In turn, I gave a great deal of freedom to my students in consultation early in my career. They were encouraged to develop their own models of consultation and to develop and try out methods for implementing their emerging models.

During the 30-year period since I began teaching consultation, I have learned a great deal about the practice of consultation and have developed firm positions about the best ways to provide consultation and research its efficacy. These strong beliefs about practice and research sometimes influence me to constrain my students' freedom by forcing them to adopt my consultation approach. As our knowledge base grows, it will become increasingly important for consultant trainers to give students sufficient freedom to develop and implement their own ideas about consultation and practitioner research. This should help to ensure that trainees will develop feelings of ownership for their ideas about consultation, use consultation long after training is complete and evaluate consultation in their own practice. There is a need for research to document these expected effects.

Multicultural Issues in Consultation

Despite the progress that has been made in developing consultation as an effective preventive intervention strategy in schools, there has been relatively little attention to cultural issues (Ingraham, 2000). The literature that does exist has focused primarily on developing models of multicultural consultation, but this has had little impact on the general literature in consultation (Ingraham, 2000). Perhaps one reason for this limited impact is that there has been little research on multicultural issues in consultation. As a result, Ingraham suggests that there are two major needs in this area: (1) to develop a comprehensive framework for practicing multicultural and cross cultural consultation; and (2) to conduct empirical research on multicultural school based consultation. Ingraham's article takes some important steps toward developing such a model, and a special issue in the *School Psychology Review* adds significantly to the empirical literature on multicultural consultation by providing several studies that use qualitative methodology (Ingraham & Meyers, 2000). That special issue argues that it is critically important that these issues are incorporated into consultation training.

Harding's (1991) work on "Strong Objectivity" provides a framework that has the potential to contribute to multicultural school based consultation and these potential contributions have been discussed recently (Henning-Stout & Meyers, 2000). Strong Objectivity provides a framework for developing strategies to reconsider accepted knowledge about consultation.

From this perspective, attempts to maintain objective research methodology by removing social values from investigations of social phenomena are limited by the social perspectives of the investigators (Harding, 1991).

Investigators asking the questions will seek (often without being aware of it) to eliminate the values that derive from perspectives that are different from the mainstream, while emphasizing their own values that will generally reflect the mainstream culture associated with consultation research. Instead of enhancing the objectivity of research, Harding argues that this adherence to mainstream values actually weakens objectivity due to the important marginalized voices that are excluded from the research.

"Harding (1991) suggests that the most untainted perspectives on any mainstream theory or practice come from those people who are most marginal to the system or culture that has generated the theory or practice" (Henning-Stout & Meyers, 2000). Thus, in consultation practice, consultation research and consultation training, it may be possible to strengthen objectivity by obtaining input from those who are marginal to the consultation system or the training system when contrasted with consultants or trainers. Relatively marginal voices in consultation include teacher-consultees, parents, students, those from minority backgrounds, graduate student trainees, and so forth. I am beginning to add this perspective to my efforts to train consultants, as I am learning to pay greater attention to consultation strategies that can be sensitive to and effective with consultees and students from a range of social, ethnic and economic backgrounds. There is a need for research addressing these issues in consultation and consultation training.

When Should Consultation Be Taught?

Throughout my career, I have struggled with the question of when consultation should be taught within a graduate student's program. Should it be taught at the masters or doctoral level and should it be taught early in the program or late in the program?

The university training programs that I have been associated with have adopted the perspective that consultation training should occur after training in psychoeducational diagnosis. The advantage of this approach is that students entering into a consultation relationship will have developed beginning expertise in psychoeducational diagnosis that might facilitate their efforts to provide consultation. This perspective often results in consultation courses being offered toward the end of a student's nondoctoral program (i.e., masters degree or specialist level training such as the EdS degree) or in a doctoral program, or both. In this context, it can be argued that offering consultation training early can be ineffective because the student may have too little expertise and experience to provide effective consultation during the practicum component of the course. Although students may learn a great deal from their mistakes, the learning may not be constructive when their efforts to apply consultation are consistently unsuccessful. This can teach ineffective consultation strategies and it can reduce the likelihood that trainees engage in consultation in the future.

Two additional factors can be influential in determining when to provide consultation training. First, how many graduate courses and how many credit hours are required to teach school-based consultation effectively? The brief discussion provided about topics that ought to be included in consultation training and a review of the supporting literature that was presented in that section of the article indicate that there is a tremendous amount of content to be included in any consultation course. It may not be possible to provide adequate training with just one three-credit course in consultation and one solution is to offer multiple courses on consultation. I teach two courses in consultation. One is a beginning level course that focuses on child-centered and consultee-centered consultation, and the second is an advanced course that is focused on organizational consultation, school change and primary prevention.

A second related factor concerns the model of training. The suggestions presented previously are based on models of training that assume psychoeducational assessment and diagnostic skills (or other basic skills based on direct service such as counseling) must be learned prior to consultation. These suggestions are also based on a training model that assumes a discrete number of courses are needed in graduate programs to teach major learning goals such as consultation (i.e., assessment, counseling, behavior management, consultation, etc.). Models of graduate training that emphasize consultation and prevention and that consider the entire training program rather than discrete courses, might view preventive intervention and consultation skills to be more important than psychoeducational diagnosis. From this perspective, consultation and preventive intervention would be viewed as skills that ought to be taught throughout the graduate program rather than being defined solely by one or even two courses.

It can be argued that beginning training with any direct service skill, such as psychoeducational diagnosis or counseling, conveys that direct service is the primary mode of service delivery, and that learning and behavior problems lie within the child rather than the environment. It may be more effective to begin training by focusing on preventive intervention and consultation. Using this framework, consultation and intervention training might begin during students' first semester and continue throughout their program. Perhaps direct service strategies should be among the last things that graduate students in education and psychology are taught.

CONCLUSIONS

Clearly, the field of school-based consultation has not paid enough attention to training. An example supporting this point is the excellent chapter on school based consultation that Terry Gutkin and Mike Curtis have written for the *Handbook of School Psychology* (Gutkin & Curtis, 1999). This chapter does a very good job of reviewing issues related to the practice of consultation and related theory and research. Despite its many strengths, this chapter does not discuss consultation training. A key aspect of our neglect of training has been the dearth of research on this topic. It is critically important that those providing consultation training develop effective strategies for conducting research about the training that they provide. This connects to the suggestion that consultants conduct research about their own practice using the "practitioner-researcher" model presented earlier. Furthermore, it must be noted that the lack of data on training raises questions about some of the conclusions that I make in this article. Clearly, there is a need for research addressing these issues, so that a systematic data base (derived from qualitative as well as quantitative data) can be used to evaluate claims such as those made in this article.

Consultation trainers need to model the role of practitioner researcher by acting as "practitioner researchers" who research their own practice of providing training about consultation. This article presents a number of challenges to training that have been factors in the field of consultation for 30 years. It is underscored that substantial attention is needed to develop approaches for research, practice and training concerning multicultural issues in consultation.

It is important to think about those things that need to be done to train consultees, yet there has been little attention to this issue. There is no reason to suspect that consultation is the sole responsibility of the consultant and that the consultee has no role in ensuring that consultation runs smoothly. It is likely that there are key areas of training for consultees that would be significant in facilitating effective consultation such as problem definition, data collection, and intervention skills (e.g., see Meyers, 1982).

This is another area that merits attention from those conducting research about consultation.

An Agenda for Research Concerning Consultation Training

I argue that there is a compelling need for research investigating the process and outcomes of training in consultation. Research is needed to determine the impact that training has on: (a) the motivation of trainees to provide an indirect service model in which they do not work directly with the client, (b) trainee knowledge and skills concerning linkages between consultation and prevention, (c) trainee knowledge and use of the consultation stages, (d) trainee knowledge and use of effective interpersonal process skills, (e) trainee knowledge and skills concerning the use of consultation in group contexts, and (f) trainee knowledge and skills concerning multicultural issues in consultation.

Research on consultation training should consider the impact of various approaches to practicum and role play on the development of relevant knowledge and skills in consultation, as well as assessing the impact of various strategies designed to produce feelings of ownership in trainees for consultation that would result in increased use of consultation strategies subsequent to training. Since practitioner–researcher skills may be particularly important to developing effective consultants and to expanding pertinent knowledge in the field, an important goal of research in consultation training should be to determine the impact of training on trainee's knowledge and use of such skills resulting in written, audiovisual, and oral research reports produced by trainees to contribute to the knowledge base in the field.

Finally, it would be constructive to consider what criteria should be used to indicate whether consultation training has been effective. One type of criterion would be to consider various outcomes in the consultant trainee such as cognitive understanding of consultation principles, use of effective interpersonal process skills when conducting consultation, effective implementation of problem solving stages, and so forth. In addition, however, I have always found that an important criterion concerning the success of consultation training has been the degree to which I have learned something from my students. When the faculty member learns from graduate students, it is likely that a successful instructional dialogue has been established that actively engaged the students. This may be an important and stimulating goal to be considered by those conducting research about consultation training.

REFERENCES

Alpert, J. L. (1983, August). *Future, prevention, change and school psychology.* Presidential address to Division 16 of the American Psychological Association at the Annual convention, Anaheim, CA.

Alpert, J. L., & Meyers, J. (Eds.). (1983). *Training in consultation: Perspectives from mental health, behavioral and organizational consultation.* Springfield, IL: Thomas.

Babinski, L. M., & Rogers, D. L. (1998). Supporting new teachers through consultee-centered group consultation. *Journal of Educational and Psychological Consultation, 9,* 285–308.

Bardon, J. I. (1982). Promoting faculty development in a college. In J. L. Alpert (Ed.), *Psychological consultation in educational settings* (pp. 174–207). San Francisco: Jossey-Bass.

Bergan, J. R., & Kratochwill, T. R. (1990). *Behavioral consultation and therapy.* New York: Plenum.

Brown, D., Pryswansky, W. B., & Schulte, A. C. (1995). *Psychological consultation: Introduction to theory and practice* (3rd ed.). Boston: Allyn & Bacon.

Brown, D., Wyne, M. D., Blackburn, J. E., & Powell, W.C. (1979). *Consultation.* Boston: Allyn & Bacon.

Caplan, G., & Caplan, R. B. (1993). *Mental health consultation and collaboration.* San Francisco: Jossey-Bass.

Cochran-Smith, M., & Lytle, S. L. (1993). *Inside outside: Teacher research and knowledge.* New York: Teachers College Press.

Cochran-Smith, M., & Lytle, S. L. (2000). The teacher research movement: A decade later. *Educational Researcher, October,* 15–25.

Conoley, J. C., & Conoley, C. W. (1992). *School consultation: Practice and training* (2nd ed.). New York: Pergamon.

Costenbader, V., Swartz, J., & Petrix, L. (1992). Consultation in the schools: The relationship between preservice training, perception of consultative skills, and actual time spent in consultation. *School Psychology Review, 21,* 95–108.

Cohern, E., & Osterweil, Z. (1986). An "issue-focused" model for mental health consultation with groups of teachers. *Journal of School Psychology, 18,* 210–221.

Dinkmeyer, D., & Carlson, J. (1973). *Consulting.* Columbus, OH: Charles E. Merrill.

Eidle, K. A., Truscott, S. D., Meyers, J., & Boyd, T. (1998). The role of prereferral intervention teams in early intervention and prevention of mental health problems. *School Psychology Review, 27,* 204–216.

Erchul, W. P. (1999). Two steps forward, one step back: Collaboration in school-based consultation. *Journal of School Psychology, 37,* 191–203.

Erchul, W. P., & Martens, B. K. (1997). *School consultation: Conceptual and empirical bases of practice* (2nd ed.). New York: Plenum.

Flugum, K. R., Reschly, D. J. (1994). Prereferral interventions: Quality indices and outcomes. *Journal-of-School-Psychology, 32,* 1–14.

Gallessich, J. (1983). Training psychologists for consultation with organizations. In J. L. Alpert & J. Meyers (Eds.), *Training in consultation: Perspectives from mental health, behavioral and organizational consultation* (pp. 142–163). Springfield, IL: Thomas.

Gutkin, T. B. (Ed.). (1997). Social psychology and consultation (Special section). *Journal of School Psychology, 35*(2), 105–216.

Gutkin, T. B. (1999). Collaborative versus directive/prescriptive/expert school-based consultation: Reviewing and resolving a false dichotomy. *Journal of School Psychology, 37*, 161–190.

Gutkin, T. B., & Conoley, J. C. (1990). Reconceptualizing school psychology from a service delivery perspective: Implications for practice, training and research. *Journal of School Psychology, 28,* 203–223.

Gutkin, T. B., & Curtis, M. J. (1999). School-based consultation theory and practice: The art and science of indirect service delivery. In C. R. Reynolds & T. B. Gutkin (Eds.), *The handbook of school psychology* (pp. 598–637). New York: Wiley.

Gutkin, T. B., & Nemeth, C. (1997). Selected factors impacting decision making in prereferral intervention and other school-based teams: Exploring the intersection between school and social psychology. *Journal of School Psychology, 35,* 195–216.

Harding, S. (1991). *Whose science? Whose Knowledge? Thinking from women's lives.* Ithaca, NY: Cornell University Press.

Hasbrouck, J. E., Parker, R. I., & Tindal, G.A. (1999). Perceptions of usefulness of case-related activities: Implications for training. *Journal of Educational and Psychological Consultation, 10,* 83–90.

Henning-Stout, M. (1994). Consultation and connected knowing: What we know is determined by the questions we ask. *Journal of Educational and Psychological Consultation, 5,* 81–97.

Henning-Stout, M., & Meyers, J. (2000). Consultation and human diversity: First things first. *School Psychology Review, 29,* 419–425.

Ingraham, C. L. (2000). Consultation through a multicultural lens: Multicultural and cross-cultural consultation in schools. *School Psychology Review, 29,* 320–343.

Ingraham, C. L., & Meyers, J. (2000). Multicultural and cross cultural consultation: Cultural diversity issues in school consultation [Special issue]. *School Psychology Review, 29,* 315–428.

Keys, C. (1983). Graduate training in organizational consultation: Three dilemmas. In J. L. Alpert & J. Meyers (Eds.), *Training in consultation: Perspectives from mental health, behavioral and organizational consultation* (pp. 123–141). Springfield, IL: Thomas.

Kressel, K., Bailey, J. R., & Forman, S.G. (1999). Psychological consultation in higher education: Lessons from a university faculty development center. *Journal of Educational and Psychological Consultation, 10,* 51–82.

LeCompte, M. D., & Schensul, J. J. (1999). *Designing and conducting ethnographic research: Ethnographer's Toolkit* (Vol. I). Walnut Creek, CA: AltaMira.

Marks, E. S. (1995). *Entry strategies for school consultation.* New York: Guilford.

Meyers, J. (1982). *Consultation skills: How teachers can maximize help from specialists in schools.* A training module prepared for the National Support Systems Project, University of Minnesota.

Meyers, J. (1995). A consultation model for school psychological services: Twenty years later. *Journal of Educational and Psychological Consultation, 6,* 73–81.

Meyers J. (1998). Should school psychology exist? Implications of prevention, research and training. In E. Gaughan & E. Faherty (Eds.), *School Psychology: Prospective and retrospective views of the field.* Alfred, NY: Lea R. Powell Institute for Children and Families at Alfred University.

Meyers, J., Brent, D., Faherty, E., & Modafferi, C. (1993). Caplan's contributions to the practice of psychology in schools. In W. P. Erchul (Ed.), *Consultation in community, school, and organizational practice: Gerald Caplan's contributions to professional psychology* (pp. 99–122). Washington, DC: Hemisphere.

Meyers, J., & Nastasi, B. K. (1999). Primary prevention in school settings. In C. R. Reynolds & T. B. Gutkin (Eds.), *The handbook of school psychology* (3rd ed., pp. 764–799). New York: Wiley.

Meyers, J., Parsons, R. D. & Martin, R. P. (1979). *Theory and practice of mental health consultation in the schools.* San Francisco: Jossey-Bass.

Meyers, B., Valentino, C. T., Meyers, J., Boretti, M., & Brent, D. (1996). Implementing prereferral intervention teams as an approach to school-based consultation in an urban school system. *Journal of Educational and Psychological Consultation, 7,* 119–149.

Parsons, R. D., & Meyers, J. (1984). *Developing consultation skills: A guide to training, development and assessment for human services professionals.* San Francisco: Jossey-Bass.

Rappaport, J. (1981). In praise of paradox: A social policy of empowerment over prevention. *American Journal of Community Psychology, 9,* 1–25.

Rosenfield, S. A., (1987). *Instructional consultation.* Hillsdale, NJ: Lawrence Erlbaum Associates, Inc.

Rosenfield, S. A., & Gravois, T. A. (1996). *Instructional consultation teams.* New York: Guilford.

Tombari, M. L., & Bergan, J. R. (1978). Consultant cues and teacher verbalizations, judgments, and expectancies concerning children's adjustment problems. *Journal of School Psychology, 16,* 212–219.

Truscott, S. D., Cosgrove, G., Meyers, J., & Eidle-Barkman K. A. (2000). The acceptability of organizational consultation with prereferral intervention teams. *School Psychology Quarterly, 15,* 172–206.

Joel Meyers is Professor in the Department of Counseling and Psychological Services and Director of Project DOVE (a school-based dropout prevention and violence prevention initiative) at Georgia State University. His research interests include mental health consultation, the primary prevention of violence and school dropout, prereferral intervention teams as a preventive approach to service delivery and school reform.

JOURNAL OF EDUCATIONAL AND PSYCHOLOGICAL CONSULTATION, 13(1&2), 55–67

Developing Nonthreatening Expertise: Thoughts on Consultation Training From the Perspective of a New Faculty Member

Adena B. Meyers

Illinois State University

A new faculty member's experiences teaching consultation for the first time are described. Several dilemmas and challenges involved in the initial planning of a consultation course are discussed, including: how to fit the consultation course into the broader school psychology training program; how to balance didactic and applied training; and how to teach the interpersonal skills necessary for students to form productive, collaborative relationships with diverse adults. It is argued that Black feminist epistemology (Collins, 2000) provides a potentially useful framework for helping students develop effective collaborative skills.

As a relatively recent graduate of a doctoral program in clinical-community psychology, and a new faculty member in the school psychology program at Illinois State University, I was both eager and apprehensive when presented with the opportunity to teach Theory and Practice of Mental Health Consultation in the Schools. Drawing on my background in clinical-community psychology, I hoped to offer the school psychology students some new ideas and perspectives, yet I wanted the course to be relevant to their interests and responsive to their training needs. While attempting to strike this balance, I also confronted dilemmas about how to fit the course into the existing curriculum, how to balance the didactic and practice components of consulta-

Correspondence should be addressed to Adena B. Meyers, Department of Psychology, Illinois State University, Campus Box 4620, Normal, IL 61790–4620. E-mail: abmeyer@ilstu.edu

tion training, and how to challenge students to develop and grow, without causing them to feel unduly threatened or become overwhelmed. This article describes some of the strategies used to resolve these dilemmas. It also presents a framework for approaching what I view as one of the most challenging and least understood aspects of consultation training: How to teach students to collaborate effectively with diverse adults.

CONSULTATION MODEL AND RELATED TRAINING OBJECTIVES

My own training and professional experience lead me to view consultation as an important part of the psychologist's role that may include such activities as advising and collaborating with community groups, parents, human service professionals (including teachers), and organizations (including schools) in an effort to assist in identifying and solving problems, gathering and interpreting relevant data, and generating, implementing, and evaluating potentially effective intervention strategies. This view of consultation is informed by a number of theoretical perspectives including organizational development (e.g., Schmuck, 1990), ecological psychology (e.g., Bronfenbrenner, 1977), empowerment (e.g., Rappaport, 1987), and behavioral problem solving (e.g., Kratochwill & Bergan, 1990). This approach is consistent with the ecobehavioral model described by Gutkin and Curtis (1999). I am particularly interested in training future school psychologists to facilitate change at the level that Bronfenbrenner labels the mesosystem, by strengthening connections between and among the various microsystems (e.g., peers, family, school, etc.) in a child's life. For example, consultation at the mesosystem level might involve helping parents and teachers to consider each others' perspectives, communicate more effectively, and work together in developing problem-solving strategies (e.g., Christensen & Hirsch, 1998; Schoenwald, Henggeler, Brondino, & Donkervoet, 1997; Sheridan, 1997).

A number of training objectives cut across these varied activities and functions, and these have provided an initial framework for my conceptualization of consultation training. Specifically, the effective consultant must be familiar with consultation theory and research, knowledgeable about behavior problems and behavior change, and sensitive to the role of contextual factors in maintaining or changing behavior. He or she must be skilled in problem solving and applied research, and in many contexts, must be able to influence his or her own job responsibilities to create opportunities for meaningful consultation (Marks, 1995). In addition, a consultant must be able to communicate effectively and develop productive working relationships with diverse adults. As Gutkin and Curtis (1999) pointed out, "Although initially given less attention by those who were focused primarily on the technology of a client's behavior change, it is becoming increasingly clear to consultation advocates of all persuasions that the person-to-person relationships established during the course of consultation mediate the effectiveness of consultation services" (p. 604). Teaching students how to develop these relationships is, in my view, one of the most important and most challenging tasks that consultation trainers face.

Planning the Course

I began my planning efforts by reviewing previous syllabi, conferring with colleagues, and speaking with advanced students who had taken the course in recent years. These inquiries helped provide a general picture of how the course had been taught in the past, and guided preliminary decisions regarding topics to cover, readings to assign, how to structure the class meetings, and how many and what type(s) of written assignments to require. In addition, on the first day of class, students were asked to provide anonymous responses to questions about their definitions of consultation, their training goals, and their feelings about engaging in supervised consultation activities. Students' answers to these questions helped shape the course as the semester unfolded.

Fitting into the existing curriculum. In our program, doctoral and specialist students are required to take consultation at the start of their second year. This course introduces the theoretical and empirical consultation literature, and also provides a supervised training component. It was thus necessary to determine how to cover the important content domains adequately and provide meaningful practice opportunities within a single semester.

One helpful strategy for coping with this challenge was to identify and build on strengths in the students' prior training. After completing the first year coursework, our students have already developed relevant skills and knowledge in the following domains: (a) a broad understanding of the various roles and functions of school psychologists, including consultation;

(b) knowledge about local and state policies and practices that are consistent with a consultation model of service delivery; (c) positive attitudes about engaging in consultation; (d) familiarity with a school setting (students spend 2 hours per week at their school placements throughout the first year of training); (e) good understanding of behavioral assessment and intervention; and (f) exposure to active listening techniques and other useful interpersonal skills.

With this background, most students entering the consultation class are interested in learning to deliver indirect services to children by consulting with teachers and parents, but feel unprepared to do so. They are eager to apply behavioral problem-solving steps (e.g., Kratochwill & Bergan, 1990) to their cases, but are unfamiliar with other theoretical approaches to consultation (e.g., mental health, systems, instructional, and group consultation). In this context, it seemed important to expose students to a range of theoretical models of consultation, but I believed that the greatest gains in relevant skills would occur if students were encouraged to use a familiar framework (i.e., behavioral problem solving) with their consultation cases. In this way, students could focus on learning to develop productive working relationships with parents and teachers.

Balancing didactic and applied components.   Striking an appropriate balance between the science and practice of consultation is a familiar challenge for trainers (Idol, 1993; Keys, 1983). Given the time constraints previously noted, my decisions about how to balance didactic instruction and skill development were particularly difficult and involved significant compromise on both ends. The result was a class essentially divided into two units, the first introductory and primarily didactic, the second more advanced and primarily applied. Specifically, students spent the beginning of the semester reading introductory material about consultation (primarily from textbooks), and engaging in simulated skill practice (primarily through role-plays). Didactic content was presented in class via lecture and guided class discussions. Students spent the latter part of the semester engaging in consultation, receiving group supervision, and reading articles on more focused or advanced topics in the field (e.g., multicultural consultation, conjoint behavioral consultation, social psychology and consultation, etc.). Students were responsible (with guidance from the instructor) for identifying relevant articles and presenting the information to each other.

Helping Students Become Nonthreatening Experts

As noted in the previous paragraphs, I believe that it is both important *and difficult* to teach new consultants how to collaborate effectively. This difficulty may stem in part from the lack of a clear operational definition of collaboration (e.g., Erchul, 1999; Gutkin, 1999) and from the related lack of sufficient empirical evidence about the elements of effective collaboration (Minke, 2000). Nevertheless, on the assumption that collaboration is at least as much an art as a science (and on the assumption that it *is* important to the consultative mission), helping students learn to collaborate effectively is one of my primary objectives as a consultation trainer.

To collaborate effectively, consultants must be able to recognize the expertise of parents and other professionals, while maintaining professional identities themselves. More an attitude than a skill per se, the importance of this stance is reflected in many statements and concepts in the consultation literature. According to Gutkin and Curtis (1999), for example, "perhaps the most common and long-standing assumption about consultant–consultee relationships is that they should be collegial and collaborative rather than hierarchical and coercive" (p. 604). Conoley and Conoley (1992) defined consultation as a relationship "among peer professionals [that] is collaborative and coordinate" (p. 2). In addition, they pointed out that (among other qualities) "preferred consultants exhibit…nonthreatening expertise" (p. 19). This appears to be a worthy training objective, but how does one teach students to exhibit nonthreatening expertise?

When they begin working in professional roles, many trainees would be better described as nonthreatening novices (who may themselves feel threatened by the expertise of others). As one student indicated at the beginning of the semester: "I hope this class will increase my confidence that I do have useful ideas and knowledge to offer other professionals. It's still difficult for me to think of myself as a 'professional' and not a student whose only role is to learn from others." Helping such students begin to recognize their own expertise may enable them to become better collaborators. On the other hand, some beginning students are so eager to be seen as experts that they may inadvertently come across as threatening or dogmatic. For example, one student worried that "Because of my inexperience within the school system, I feel some teachers may not respect my advice as much as I would like." To avoid appearing overconfident, students who share this view may improve as consultants if they can learn to recognize and respect expertise in others.

Mainstream consultation texts (e.g., Conoley & Conoley, 1992) describe a number of useful strategies for striking this balance between confidence and deference in the consultative relationship. These include: use of one-downsmanship; being indirect when necessary; giving credit to the consultee whenever possible; and use of referent power (i.e., increasing the credibility of the consultant's suggestions by emphasizing similarities between the consultant and consultee). Though clearly important and helpful, each of these strategies poses potential problems, particularly when implemented by inexperienced consultants. For example, if used disingenuously, strategies such as one-downsmanship and giving credit to the consultee could come across as condescending (Reyes & Jason, 1993). Among some cultural groups these strategies may even cause discomfort and thus be less effective than a more directive approach (Tarver Behring, Cabello, Kushida, & Murguia, 2000). Similarly, although the use of referent power provides a viable alternative for young consultants struggling to establish expert power, referent power depends on the consultee's perception of similarity between self and consultant (Erchul & Raven, 1997; Martin, 1978). This may be difficult to establish when in fact the consultant and consultee have little in common. As challenging as these issues are for trainees consulting with teachers or other professionals, they are potentially even more problematic when consulting with parents, who typically represent a very wide range of socioeconomic and educational backgrounds, and may feel like outsiders in the school context (Sheridan, 2000).

Part of the difficulty inherent in the "coordinate" or "collaborative" approach is that it assumes equality when in fact obvious or subtle power differentials always exist between consultant and consultee. For example, differences in educational level, organizational status, or salary may influence the relationship between school psychologist and teacher (or between teacher and consultant-in-training), while much more blatant differences in status or power are often present between consultant and parent. All of these relationship dimensions are further complicated when the members of the consultation dyad (or triad) represent different ethnic groups and/or different genders (Ingraham, 2000; Tarver Behring et al., 2000). Factors such as age and experience also come into play. Consulting with a teacher who is a 30-year veteran is different from consulting with a 20-year-old beginning his or her first teaching job. Similarly, the personal and professional backgrounds of trainees influence their experiences as beginning consultants. For example, student consultants who are parents, or who have worked as teachers, bring to the table various forms of expertise that will undoubtedly be valued more by some consultees than by others.

Black Feminist Epistemology and the Collaborative Process

How we define and evaluate expertise in the context of power differentials seems to be central to the collaborative process. One of my goals as an instructor is to help consultants-in-training develop the ability to recognize and appreciate different forms of expertise in themselves and others. To encourage students to explore various definitions and sources of expert knowledge, I assign a chapter by sociologist, Patricia Hill Collins (2000, chap. 11) entitled "Black Feminist Epistemology," in which the author distinguished standards of knowledge validation observed among African American women from the more mainstream epistemological standards of traditional social science (i.e., logical positivism). Students are thus encouraged to reconsider the privileged status of the scientific method as the "gold standard" for developing knowledge and evaluating truth claims. I believe that such questioning is a crucial first step in the process of learning to collaborate with diverse adults whose various cultural backgrounds, life experiences, and professional training may be the basis of epistemological assumptions with which the traditionally trained student is unfamiliar.

Collins (2000) described four dimensions or "contours" of Black feminist epistemology: (a) Lived Experience as a Criterion of Meaning; (b) The Use of Dialogue in Assessing Knowledge Claims; (c) The Ethic of Caring; and (d) The Ethic of Personal Accountability. Each of these epistemological dimensions sheds light on the process of collaboration among diverse experts, and each has implications for consultation training.

Lived experience as a criterion of meaning. This criterion concerns the difference between wisdom and knowledge. It questions knowledge claims made by those who have extensive "book learning" but lack "mother wit" or common sense. The implications of this criterion were articulated clearly by a woman quoted by Collins (2000): "I might not know how to use 34 words where three would do, but that does not mean that I don't know what I'm talking about... I know what I'm talking about because I'm talking about myself. I'm talking about what I have lived" (p. 258).

In the context of consultation training, I encourage students to acknowledge lived experience as one legitimate basis of expertise. For example, consider a student providing consultation to a veteran teacher who views positive reinforcement as bribery, and is thus reluctant to use this strategy in the classroom. The novice consultant, who is likely to be familiar and comfortable with behavior modification principles, may view the teacher as old fashioned or rigid and may thus have difficulty developing a productive consultative relationship. The student who assumes there is wisdom behind the teacher's views is likely to be more effective than the student who simply dismisses the teacher as "set in his/her ways" or "resistant" to consultation.

Conversely, the criterion of lived experience also implies that students need not be intimidated or silenced by their status as trainees. Students can be reminded that their own lives are valid sources of information and ideas that may be quite relevant to their consultation cases. I encourage students to identify and draw on their professional experiences (e.g., as child care providers, substitute teachers, camp counselors, etc.) and their personal experiences (e.g., as parents, relatives of children with disabilities, former elementary school students, etc.) as well as their prior coursework. In this way, they may begin to view themselves as legitimate experts who are able to participate meaningfully in the collaborative process of consultation with other experts.

The use of dialogue in assessing knowledge claims.   The reciprocal and respectful exchange of views that is so central to consultation also characterizes the second component of Collins's (2000) Black Feminist Epistemology: The use of dialogue in assessing knowledge claims. Collins explained that "For Black women new knowledge claims are rarely worked out in isolation from other individuals and are usually developed through dialogues with other members of a community" (p. 260). She emphasized that knowledge is validated in a context of interpersonal connectedness. This suggests that consultants-in-training should be encouraged to check out their hypotheses and conclusions with consultees as part of the validation process. This is similar to the technique of *member checking* used by qualitative researchers (e.g., Lincoln & Guba, 1985). For example, if a novice consultant observes a behavioral pattern in the classroom, the consultant should present it to the consultee for interpretation, discussion, and validation, not as a foregone conclusion. In many instances, checking with the child would also be advisable. Conversely, a consultee may *think* he/she knows the cause of a child's behavioral or learning problem, but given the opportunity to dialogue with others (including parents, child, *and consultant*) may ultimately improve the validity of that knowledge.

As another African American feminist scholar, Bell Hooks (1989, cited in Collins, 2000, p. 260) pointed out, "Dialogue implies talk between two subjects, not the speech of subject and object. It is a humanizing speech, one that challenges and resists domination." Collins distinguished this from what she described as a more mainstream approach to discourse involving "adversarial debate." Consultation training typically introduces students to strategies that may seem adversarial, such as confrontation (Conoley & Conoley, 1992; Kurpuis & Rozecki, 1993), and dissent (Gutkin & Nemeth 1997). Collins's view of dialogue as respectful and humanizing underscores for students that productive dialogue is not adversarial. Indeed, if conflict occurs in the context of a respectful and caring relationship, it may be more tolerable for both parties and may ultimately lead to clearer truths (see Minke, 2000, for a discussion of productive use of conflict in the context of collaborative relationships; see Rosenfield, this issue, for another perspective on the role of dialogue in creating new meaning in the context of consultation).

The ethic of caring. In contrast to the traditional social scientific approach in which objectivity is of utmost importance, Collins (2000) discussed the value that African American women place on subjective experience, emotions, and empathy in their assessment of knowledge claims. She explained, "Emotion indicates that the speaker believes in the validity of an argument" (p. 263). This is consistent with the notion that the consultant must be genuine and empathic, speaking and behaving in a way that is congruent with his or her feelings (e.g., Conoley & Conoley, 1992; Gutkin & Curtis, 1999; Kurpius & Rozecki, 1993).

In the tradition of mental health consultation, identification with the client is often seen as a problem to be corrected, as it can interfere with professional objectivity and can, in turn, be a source of ineffectiveness. The ethic of caring reminds us that there may be occasions in which identification with the client can also be helpful. In contrast with the social scientific tradition that assumes it is necessary to remain detached and unemotional to avoid bias, the ethic of caring values emotional expressiveness and suggests that the more one cares about something, the better he or she understands it. From this perspective, the views of a concerned parent might be considered more valid than those of a more "objective" teacher or consultant. Furthermore, whereas mainstream social science views subjective or personal perspectives as a source of bias, Black feminist epistemology values the uniqueness of each knower and assumes that clearer truth is obtained through the integration of multiple subjective voices. This perspective is consistent with the concept of strong objectivity, and may be applied in similar ways to the process of consultation (see Henning-Stout & Meyers, 2000; J. Meyers, this issue).

The ethic of personal accountability.   In describing the fourth component of Black feminist epistemology, Collins (2000) posited that "Assessments of an individual's knowledge claims simultaneously evaluate an individual's character, values, and ethics…All views expressed and actions
taken are thought to derive from a central set of core beliefs that cannot be
other than personal" (p. 265). A person's identity is thus viewed as relevant
to the validity of his or her claim to know something.

On the one hand, acknowledging this criterion may tap into the consultant-in-training's worst fears, as it becomes fair game for consultees to ask:
"Who are *you* to tell *me* what to do in my classroom (or how to interact with
my child)?" Instead of hiding behind a shield of scientific knowledge and
detached objectivity, my hope is that students will think hard about this
question and come up with genuine answers that they can incorporate into
their developing personal and professional identities. The answers should
be unique for each consultant, and should address his or her reasons for
entering a helping profession, wanting to help children, and choosing to
work with teachers and parents in schools. Helping students to clarify
their values, attitudes, and beliefs in this way is recognized as an important objective of consultation training (Kurpius & Lewis, 1988; Rosenfield
& Gravois, 1993).

Recent controversy in the consultation literature raises questions about
whether (or to what extent) consultation is a coercive enterprise (e.g.,
Erchul, 1999; Gutkin, 1999). For example, Erchul argued that even self-pro-
claimed nondirective consultants ultimately hope that the consultee will
"buy into" their suggestions. Even under the assumption that consultation
always does involve a degree of manipulation, the ethics of caring and of
personal accountability legitimate questions about the consultant's mo-
tives for engaging in this manipulation. *Why* do we want consultees to
"buy into" our suggestions? Is it because we like power? Because we think
we are superior to teachers and parents? Because we think we have something of value to offer that will benefit children? The ethic of personal accountability suggests that answers to questions like these matter
enormously. The acceptability of consultant directiveness or influence
may be a function of the consultee's assessment of the consultant's personal accountability for his or her suggestions.

CONCLUSION

As a new member of the consultation training community, I have outlined
my current thinking about a rationale and potential techniques for teaching

students to be collaborative consultants. Central to my working definition of collaboration is the ability to recognize and appreciate expertise in oneself and others. With this in mind, an important aim of consultation training is to help students grow into the role of nonthreatening expert by developing increasing comfort with their own expert knowledge and learning to respect the expertise of consultees without feeling threatened by it.

Collins's (2000) discussion of Black feminist epistemology provided a framework for thinking about the meaning of expertise from a collaborative point of view. By presenting this framework to students, I hope to facilitate the development of their professional identities and increase their theoretical understanding of the collaborative process. In addition, a number of potentially useful teaching methods emerge from the application of Black feminist epistemology to consultation training. For example, reminding students about the relevance of their own lived experiences might help build confidence, while encouraging students to engage in self-examination may lead to increased personal accountability, thus enhancing students' credibility as consultants. Although the effectiveness of these teaching strategies has not been established empirically, it is hoped that future research might shed light on the potential contribution of epistemological theory to consultation training and practice.

REFERENCES

Bronfenbrenner, U. (1977). Toward an experimental ecology of human development. *American Psychologist, 32*, 513–531.

Christensen, S. L., & Hirsch, J. A. (1998). Facilitating partnerships and conflict resolution between families and schools. In K. C. Stoiber & T.R. Kratochwill (Eds.), *Handbook of group intervention for children and families* (pp. 307–344). Boston: Allyn & Bacon.

Collins, P. H. (2000). *Black feminist thought: Knowledge, consciousness, and the politics of empowerment* (2nd ed.). New York: Routledge.

Conoley, J. C., & Conoley, C. W. (1992). *School consultation: Practice and training* (2nd ed.). Needham Heights, MA: Allyn & Bacon.

Erchul, W. P. (1999). Two steps forward, one step back: Collaboration in school-based consultation. *Journal of School Psychology, 37*, 191–203.

Erchul, W. P., & Raven, B. H. (1997). Social power in school consultation. A contemporary view of French and Raven's bases of power model. *Journal of School Psychology, 35*, 137–171.

Gutkin, T. B. (1999). Collaborative versus directive/prescriptive/expert school-based consultation: Reviewing and resolving a false dichotomy. *Journal of School Psychology, 37*, 161–190.

Gutkin, T. B., & Curtis, M. J. (1999). School-based consultation theory and practice: The art and science of indirect service delivery. In C. R. Reynolds & T. B. Gutkin (Eds.), *The handbook of school psychology* (3rd ed., pp. 598–637). New York: Wiley.

Gutkin, T. B., & Nemeth, C. (1997). Selected factors impacting decision-making in prereferral intervention and other school-based teams: Exploring the intersection between school and social psychology. *Journal of School Psychology, 35,* 195–216.

Henning-Stout, M., & Meyers, J. (2000). Consultation and human diversity: First things first. *School Psychology Review, 29,* 419–425.

Idol, L. (1993). Preservice education and professional staff development. In J. E. Zins, T. R. Kratochwill, & S. N. Elliott (Eds.), *Handbook of consultation services for children: Applications in educational and clinical settings* (pp. 351–372). San Francisco: Jossey-Bass.

Ingraham, C. L. (2000). Consultation through a multicultural lens: Multicultural and cross-cultural consultation in schools. *School Psychology Review, 29,* 320–343.

Keys, C. B. (1983). Graduate training in organizational consultation: Three dilemmas. In J. L. Alpert & J. Meyers (Eds.), *Training in consultation: Perspectives from mental health, behavioral, and organizational consultation* (pp. 123–141). Springfield, IL: Thomas.

Kratochwill, T. R., & Bergan, J. R. (1990). *Behavioral consultation in applied settings: An individual guide.* New York: Plenum.

Kurpius, D. J., & Lewis, J. E. (1988). Assumptions and operating principles for preparing professionals to function as consultants. In J. F. West (Ed.), *School consultation: Interdisciplinary perspectives on theory, research, training, and practice* (pp. 143–154). Austin, TX: Association of Educational and Psychological Consultants.

Kurpius, D. J., & Rozecki, T. G. (1993). Strategies for improving interpersonal communication. In J. E. Zins, T. R. Kratochwill, & S. N. Elliott (Eds.), *Handbook of consultation services for children: Applications in educational and clinical settings* (pp. 137–158). San Francisco: Jossey-Bass.

Lincoln, Y. S., & Guba, E. G. (1985). *Naturalistic inquiry.* Beverly Hills, CA: Sage.

Marks, E. S. (1995). *Entry strategies for school consultation.* New York: Guilford.

Martin, R. P. (1978). Expert and referent power: A framework for understanding and maximizing consultation effectiveness. *Journal of School Psychology, 16,* 49–55.

Minke, K. M. (2000). Preventing school problems & promoting school success through family-school-community collaboration. In Minke, K. M. & Bear, G. C. (Eds.), *Preventing school problems–promoting school success: Strategies and programs that work* (pp. 377–420). Bethesda, MD: National Association of School Psychologists.

Rappaport, J. (1987). Terms of empowerment/exemplars of prevention: Toward a theory for community psychology. *American Journal of Community Psychology, 15,* 121–148.

Reyes, O., & Jason, L. A. (1993). Collaborating with the community. In J. E. Zins, T. R. Kratochwill, & S. N. Elliott (Eds.), *Handbook of consultation services for children: Applications in educational and clinical settings* (pp. 305–316). San Francisco: Jossey-Bass.

Rosenfield, S., & Gravois, T. A. (1993). Educating consultants for applied clinical and educational settings. In J. E. Zins, T. R. Kratochwill, & S. N. Elliott (Eds.), *Handbook of consultation services for children: Applications in educational and clinical settings* (pp.373–393). San Francisco: Jossey-Bass.

Schmuck, R. (1990). Organizational development in the schools: Contemporary concepts and practices. In T. B. Gutkin & C. R. Reynolds (Eds.), *The handbook of school psychology* (2nd ed., pp. 899–919). New York: Wiley.

Schoenwald, S. K., Henggeler, S. W., Brondino, M. J., & Donkervoet, J. C. (1997). Reconnecting schools with families of juvenile offenders. In J. L. Swartz & W. E. Martin (Eds.), *Applied ecological psychology for schools within communities: Assessment and intervention* (pp. 187–205). Mahwah, NJ: Lawrence Erlbaum Associates, Inc.

Sheridan, S. M. (1997). Conceptual and empirical bases on conjoint behavioral consultation. *School Psychology Quarterly, 12,* 119–133.

Sheridan, S. M. (2000). Considerations of multiculturalism and diversity in behavioral consultation with parents and teachers. *School Psychology Review, 29,* 344–353.
Tarver Behring, S., Cabello, B., Kushida, D., & Murguia, A. (2000). Cultural modifications to current school-based consultation approaches reported by culturally diverse beginning consultants. *School Psychology Review, 29,* 354–367.

Adena B. Meyers is Assistant Professor, Department of Psychology, Illinois State University. Her research interests include adolescent pregnancy and parenthood; child maltreatment; family, school, and community interventions; graduate training in applied psychology.

JOURNAL OF EDUCATIONAL AND PSYCHOLOGICAL CONSULTATION, 13(1&2), 69–95
Copyright © 2002, Lawrence Erlbaum Associates, Inc.

Expanding Problem-Solving Consultation Training: Prospects and Frameworks

Thomas R. Kratochwill

University of Wisconsin-Madison

Paul H. Pittman

Indiana University Southeast

Core characteristics of problem-solving consultation research, theory, and practice in psychology and education are reevaluated within the context of consultation training agendas. Features of problem-solving consultation must be reconceptualized for advances to occur in future consultation training. Specifically, the consultant–consultee relationship, coordinate power status, consultee's right to reject the consultant's suggestions, involvement of the consultee in the consultation process, the voluntary nature of consultation, and ethical issues are discussed within a broadened framework for consultation training that emphasizes a process in which consultation services can occur on a variety of consultee–client dimensions. These dimensions include case-centered consultation (e.g., teacher-based consultation, parent-based consultation, conjoint parent–teacher consultation, child-based consultation, and peer-mediated consultation), technology training with teachers and parents, and organizational consultation. The expanded conceptual framework for consultation involves not only a reconceptualization of traditional problem-solving consultation core characteristics for practice, but also agendas for new areas within consultation training curricula at both the preservice and inservice levels. Moreover, such a broadened framework

Correspondence should be addressed to Thomas R. Kratochwill, School Psychology Program, 1025 West Johnson Street, University of Wisconsin–Madison, Madison WI 53706–1796.
E-mail: tomkat@education.wisc.edu

demonstrates the necessity for incorporating empirical research from other areas of psychology, education, and organizational management within the area of school consultation.

The focus of this article is on training and education issues for behavioral or problem-solving consultation. Although these terms are sometimes used synonymously, the term *"problem-solving consultation"* is preferred because it expands the conceptual framework for consultation (see Kratochwill, Elliott, & Stoiber, 2002). This article does not concern the specific techniques of training nor the outcomes of training research since that literature has been reviewed previously (see Kratochwill, Sheridan, Carrington-Rotto, & Salmon, 1992; Lepage, Kratochwill, & Elliott, 2002). The article is about (a) expanding the framework for how problem-solving consultation is defined, (b) conceptual issues that need to be considered, and ultimately, and (c) the content of what consultants must be exposed to in graduate training programs. Although consultation continues to be fundamental to applied professions such as psychology, education, and business, its core constructs need to be reconceptualized within the context of various options for service delivery. Reconceptualization of core constructs in problem-solving consultation is essential for several reasons. The reasons stem from such characteristics as the increased emphasis on consultation in graduate training programs, the linkage of consultation with alternative assessment and intervention practices among psychologists, educators, and organizational consultants, the potential for consultation to incorporate a prevention focus in research and practice, and the high interest in comparative outcome research across the various consultation models represented in theory and research (Kratochwill, Sheridan, & VanSomeren, 1988; Kratochwill et al., 1992).

Several important training concerns emerge in the problem-solving consultation literature that must be addressed for some basic advances to be made in graduate education. First, the consultation literature in school psychology has been in general, too limited. Many studies that feature consultation service delivery models (or what are called mediator-based services within the literature on teacher and parent intervention) are typically not considered within the domain of outcome research within consultation in the professions of school psychology and special education.[1] For exam-

---

[1]These trends are not surprising given the finding that school psychology journals give and receive communication mostly to each other (e.g., Frisby, 1998). In other words, authors cite the literature within the field of school psychology as represented in the school psychology journal.

ple, a number of studies have been published in the applied behavior analysis literature that feature "consultation models" with teachers and/or parents (see, e.g., the *Journal of Applied Behavior Analysis*). Outside the profession of school psychology, consultation is conceptualized as an indirect service approach linked, for example, to community mental health (e.g., Schulberg & Jerrell, 1983) and is not discussed as an approach separate from any other form of child psychotherapy. In fact, "consultation" and the literature attesting to its efficacy (i.e., literature reviews, metaanalysis) are not even mentioned in Kazdin's (1988) classic work on developing effective child treatments, although a number of indirect treatments with parents and teachers were reviewed. Perhaps researchers and writers in other professions do not prioritize the service delivery features of interventions, but rather focus on the treatment itself (e.g., parent training to treat aggressive behavior).

Second, perhaps through tradition, convention, or the association of consultation in school psychology practices in educational settings, consultation research in education and psychology has primarily focused on teachers as consultees. This focus has limited the scope of discussions on issues such as collaboration; coordinate power status, and so forth, within the consultation field. Thus, when parents, students, and the "system" are considered as consultees in the problem solving process, the features that define the *process of consultation* can be expanded.

Third, there continues to be debate about research and research outcomes. For example, there is debate over how trustworthy the research base is that supports the efficacy of consultation. The issues of design and integrity are also raised (e.g., Gresham, 1989) and controversy surrounds the range of outcome measures that might be invoked within consultation research (Watson, Sterling, & McDade, 1997). One of the important issues that must be addressed is the type of evidence-based interventions that can be used across various mediators within a consultation service delivery context.

A FRAMEWORK FOR PROBLEM-SOLVING CONSULTATION TRAINING

Almost since the inception of psychology, education, and business/organizational theory, research and practice consultation has been a part of these fields. Scholars have spent time incorporating consultation within training programs, developing guidelines for practice, and have channeled energies into supporting conceptual and methodological developments in the field. Consultation represents a model for the delivery of intervention services within the broader domain of mental health and/or educational services to children and adolescents (Kratochwill et al., in press; Roberts et al., 1998). With pleas over the years for a broadened indirect service delivery role (e.g., Conoley & Gutkin, 1986; Stewart, 1986), the conceptual framework for theory, research, and practice in consultation remains a subject of considerable discussion (Kratochwill, Bergan, Sheridan, & Elliott, 1998; Noell, Gresham, & Duhon, 1998; Noell & Witt, 1996; Watson et al., 1997).

Kratochwill and his associates (see Kratochwill et al., 1992) emphasized that consultation practice is broad, taking into account at least three types of approaches to services in mental health and educational settings (see also Kratochwill et al., 1998; Kratochwill & Bergan, 1990; Kratochwill, Sladeczek, & Plunge, 1995). Because these approaches are reviewed in detail elsewhere, they will only be mentioned briefly here. In traditional case-centered approaches to consultation, the consultant works through a consultee to serve a client. The majority of the research on consultation in schools has focused on case-centered models, although most of the research is with teachers.

A second form of indirect service delivery involving consultee skill development has been labeled "technology training" (Vernberg & Reppucci, 1986), which bears similarity to consultee-centered case consultation in mental health consultation (Caplan & Caplan, 1993). Within this framework, consultation involves training parents and/or teachers during the consultation process. Several illustrations of this form of consultation have been provided in the school psychology research literature (e.g., Rhoades & Kratochwill, 1998; Rotto & Kratochwill, 1994). The applications are extensive in the clinical child literature such as in the domain of parent training.

A third dimension of consultation involves the organizational level or what can be considered a system-based consultation focus (e.g., Ikeda, Tilly, Stumme, Volmer, & Allison, 1996; Sugai & Horner, 1999). Organizational consultation, which has part of its tradition in business and organizational management fields, involves a variety of issues that extend beyond case-centered and technology training to areas such as group dynamics, organizational structure, and group problem solving. Nevertheless, the consultation problem-solving process can be invoked when this model is adopted in research and practice. This dimension of consultation training in graduate training is especially important given the focus on organizational change, conflict resolution, and system reform.

Kratochwill et al. (1992) provided an overview of current research on behavioral consultation training within the aforementioned framework for both preservice and inservice training. It is noteworthy that consultation training studies evolved from early work focused on specific consultation skills to more recent work that involves more comprehensive training and assessment of skills in actual consultation casework (e.g., Kratochwill, Elliott, & Busse, 1995; Lepage et al., 2002). Two studies that feature case-centered training are mentioned briefly because they were not reviewed previously. In the Kratochwill et al. (1995) study, researchers evaluated a 5-year, competency-based consultation training program with measures of consultant change, client outcomes, and consumer satisfaction. Written assessments of knowledge and attitudes, audio taped measures of consultation skills, behavior observations of students, and written evaluations were used to assess the training program. Results indicated consultants' knowledge and skills increased with training more than with the no-training control group and remained high during generalization. Furthermore, client outcome goals were obtained, in some cases, and participants reported overall satisfaction with training and services.

The Lepage et al. (2002) research project replicates Kratochwill et al.'s (1995) study. Assessments of consultants, clients, and consumer satisfaction were used to examine the effects of a competency-based consultation training program conducted over a 4-year period. Using a multiple baseline framework to assess training effects on consultants and single-participant designs to evaluate changes in client behavior, a number of results were found. Consultants increased their consultation skills and knowledge, but reported no change in attitudes toward behavioral intervention techniques. Supervised consultation with preschool teachers and parents resulted in a range of behavior change in clients with an overall affect size of 0.51. Consumers reported a high level of satisfaction with training and consultation services. Results of a long-term follow-up with consultants indicated positive views and use of consultation.

As illustrated in both this training research and in several major textbooks in the field of psychology (e.g., Bergan & Kratochwill, 1990), the indirect service delivery component is one of the major identifying features of consultation. Consultants work indirectly with a consultee, but as noted by Gutkin and Curtis (1999), other alignments are possible. The possibilities include several dimensions that are workable alternatives in research and practice, but not commonly elucidated in the consultation training research literature. On close examination, however, research has occurred involving the application of these indirect service approaches and therefore, training agendas in preservice graduate and inservice training in these domains must be considered. Table 1 presents several optional consultation services along with definitions and illustrations of each approach

TABLE 1
Alternative Consultation Relationship

Consultee-Mediator	Definition
Case-centered consultation	
Teacher-based consultation	Teacher serves in the role as mediator in service delivery.
Parent-based consultation	Parent serves in the role as mediator in service delivery.
Conjoint consultation: Teacher-parent	Teacher and parent(s) share a joint responsibility in the role as mediator in service delivery.
Child-based consultation	Child serves in the role of mediator in service delivery with adults.
Peer-mediated consultation	Child serves in the role of mediator in service delivery with peers.
Technology training/consultation	
Teacher training	Teacher serves in the role as mediator and is trained in the intervention and/or service delivery.
Parent training	Parent serves in the role as mediator and is trained in the intervention and/or service delivery.
Organizational consultation	
System-level consultation	System-change agents serve in the roles as mediator in service delivery.

used in practice. Each of these domains is presented briefly following and is then revisited later in the article within the context of consultation core characteristics and implications for training.

Case-Centered Consultation

Teacher-based consultation. Teacher mediated intervention is one of the most frequently adopted models of conducting school-based consultation, in part, due to tradition and issues related to the obvious availability of teachers as intervention agents in educational settings. Most consultation research in the profession of school psychology has been conducted with teachers. Moreover, most of the consultation focuses on elementary as opposed to high school activities. For example, Fuchs, Fuchs, Dulan, Roberts, and Fernstrom (1992) found that 77 studies focused on mainstream kindergarten through eighth grade settings while only 9 concentrated on grades

9–12. The point for mentioning teacher-based case consultation is that most of our cherished constructs in consultation training are derived from this literature and conceptual framework. Issues such as coordinate power status, relationship issues, and our analyses of process (discussed later in the article) are nested within (and are often limited to) this traditional case-centered domain.

Parent-based consultation.   Consulting with parents has been increasingly recognized as a viable option within the field of school psychology, although core characteristics of consultation pertaining to specific procedures with parents is not as well articulated in the consultation research literature. A large and growing body of research has incorporated a parent consultation focus within the application of behavior analysis in educational settings. With the exception of a few authors historically describing these applications as "parent consultation" (e.g., Cobb & Medway, 1978; Ollendick & Cerny, 1981), much of this work is not specifically discussed within the mainstream of school consultation literature.

Consider, for example, that researchers and writers in the school consultation field have often neglected to utilize the available evidence-based literature in applied behavior analysis as an illustration of effective research outcomes in consultation generally. Research appearing in the *Journal of Applied Behavior Analysis* since 1978 and articles in the journal *Behavior Therapy* or *Behavior Modification* contain numerous illustrations of parent consultation strategies. Although this work typically is not formally identified as "consultation," in reality, it is readily identifiable as an indirect service delivery process that corresponds to the traditional problem solving process presented by Bergan (1977) and outlined by Tharp and Wetzel (1969). In Tharp and Wetzel's work, the indirect service delivery approach with parents was conceptualized as occurring in community settings, even though a strong linkage with the school environment was recognized. Again, drawing attention to this literature emphasizes that although an important empirical base has developed in working with parent consultees, this domain is often not conceptualized as a part of school consultation research and training activities.

Conjoint consultation (parent–teacher).   It is only within approximately the past decade that researchers focused on the process of conducting consultation with both parents and teachers serving in the role as joint consultees. One early illustration involves a study by Sheridan,

Kratochwill, and Elliott (1990) in which conjoint consultation was the service delivery model. The conjoint model of consultation provides a framework that needs to be addressed in professional training such as communicating between home and school settings, increasing treatment strength, and promoting generalization of treatment effects across time (Sheridan, Kratochwill, & Bergan, 1996). Conjoint consultation can be extended to more than one parent although research has not explored certain issues related to this consultation format, such as dimensions of communication patterns. Even though gaps in our knowledge occur in this area of consultation training, there have been some conceptual advances in some areas such as multiculturalism and diversity (e.g., Ramirez, Lepage, Kratochwill, & Duffy, 1998; Sheridan, 2000).

Child-based consultation.   Most research reports in school-based consultation involve an adult consultee working with a child identified in need of some type of services. This consultant-to-consultee-to-child service delivery approach might be limited in view of our understanding of the role that children play in influencing adult behavior. For example, researchers have historically explored the effect that children have on adult behavior (see, Carr, Taylor, & Robinson, 1991; Emery, Binkoff, Houts, & Carr, 1983). The significant effect that children have on adult behavior has been identified in the developmental literature as "child effects" (Bell & Harper, 1977; Hetherington & Parke, 1986). Mentioning this research area in the context of a consultation training curriculum is warranted because children often can change adult behavior, cognition, and affect. However, having children serve as consultees has been frequently overlooked as an option for interventions through consultation, despite the potential importance of this area.

An early report in which the child was the change agent or served in the role of the consultee is illustrated in research by Graubard, Rosenberg, and Miller (1971). In a series of studies the authors taught special class students to change the behavior of teachers. Specifically, the children were taught to nod and praise the teacher contingent on teacher attention and help. In the case of negative teacher behavior the students were taught to break eye contact during teacher activities such as scolding and to ignore other kinds of provocations. The authors found that there was an increase in positive student teacher contacts and a decrease in the frequency of negative contacts. This focus on children obviously raises new possibilities in terms of traditional approaches in dealing with "resistance" in school-based consultation where authors have pointed to options that involve the teacher as a target of consultation strategies to change resistance (e.g., Witt, 1990). Alternatively, using the child as an agent of behavior change to overcome resistance factors becomes a possibility.

Carr and his associates (1991) explored the child effects concept in which 12 adults were asked to teach four pairs of children. Within each pair, one child exhibited problem behaviors and the other child did not exhibit such behaviors. The authors found that the problem children displayed negative behaviors (e.g., tantrums, aggression, and self-injury) contingent on adult instructional attempts, but not at other times whereas the nonproblem children demonstrated no problem behavior at any time. Of interest, adults who engaged in teaching activities with the nonproblem children did so with greater frequency than with the problem children. Moreover, when the adult worked with the problem child the breadth of instruction was more limited and usually involved those tasks associated with lower rates of behavior problems. This study illustrates the importance of reciprocal influences between child and adult. Furthermore, it illustrates the generative nature of the child–adult relationship to escalate in both positively and negatively reinforcing cycles. By applying the framework of reciprocal influence to consultation, there may be significant advantages in treatment planning.

Peer-mediated consultation.   Another option in consultation services incorporates having children serve as mediators for changing the behavior of their peers. Research on peer mediated intervention has traditionally been organized into three major areas including peers as tutors, peers as reinforcing agents, and peers as facilitators of generalization (Kalfus, 1984). A recent framework presented by Topping and Ehly (2001) expanded the types of "peer assisted learning" to peer tutoring, peer modeling, peer monitoring, and peer assessment. In the area of tutoring, student peer consultees might provide instructions to a student, provide correct responses, praise, deliver corrective feedback, or even ignore specific negative student behavior. Both same age and cross-age peers have been used in tutoring programs focusing on both academic and nonacademic behavior. As an early illustration, Lovitt, Lovitt, Eaton, and Kirkwood (1973) reported a study designed to treat a 9-year-old boy in a special education class who made inappropriate sexual verbalizations. In this case the children in the investigation served as passive treatment agents in the sense that physical proximity of a peer, such as sitting nearby versus moving away, was the independent variable under investigation. The treatment, reducing physical proximity, resulted in a reduction of inappropriate verbalizations by the target child and an increase in appropriate verbalizations.

Peers have also served as reinforcing agents for other children. For example, Axelrod, Hall, and Maxwell (1972) demonstrated that the study behavior of a fourth grade child could be improved as a function of peer-delivered contingent social praise. Peer-delivered social praise would be an especially useful strategy in programs designed to teach social skills.

Peers have also served as facilitators of generalization for both academic and nonacademic behavior. McKenzie and Budd (1981) explored generalized math computation of adolescents. The authors used instructions, role play, corrective feedback, and praise to train the peer tutor. During tutoring sessions, the peer tutor provided corrective feedback and delivered reinforcement to the student. The results of the investigation suggested that the tutor's presence did not serve to facilitate generalized academic responding. The authors found improvement in untrained behavior such as disruptive and on-task performance in addition to the academic measures reported during the training phase.

Using peers as mediators of behavior change for applications in educational settings opens up new possibilities for consultation services (Topping & Ehly, 2001) and training of consultants. The availability of optimal intervention programs within consultation should also spark renewed interest in considering the cost effectiveness of various intervention approaches. Peer mediated programs may allow the adult increased time for other activities (Kalfus, 1984). Peers serving in the role of consultee may also provide individualized attention to child consultees and the opportunity to learn new skills as a result of participating in the process. In addition, peers as consultees may be less threatening and more acceptable to the client and, therefore, potentially increase the effectiveness of treatment. Moreover, peers can be used to facilitate generalization and maintenance of behavior change. Whether the peer is as effective as a teacher in implementing a program and whether such processes require more or less time from consultants, teachers, and parents remains to be determined. Topping and Ehly (2001) presented some organizational and conceptual frameworks for practice.

Technology Training Consultation

As presented by Vernberg and Reppucci (1986), one option for services within problem-solving consultation is technology training, in which the consultant promotes development of skill levels in mediators or consultees who interact with clients. In the mental health consultation tradition of Caplan and Caplan (1993), this form of consultation services is called *consultee-centered case consultation*, although the mental health focus extends beyond knowledge and skill development of the consultee. Watson and Robinson (1996) revised the option for direct services to the consultee as part of a consultation relationship calling this approach *direct behavioral consultation*. They discussed the areas of direct consultation as involving several dimensions through the conventional problem solving process. For example, in the problem identification phase the consultant might model data collection, coach the consultee on data collection, as well as help establish goals. During problem analysis, the consultant might directly become involved in modeling a functional assessment as well as coaching the consultee on this type of problem solving. In plan implementation the consultant takes an active role in modeling the treatment and coaching the consultee in treatment implementation. Such implementation can improve treatment integrity and consultee skills.

Teaching technology training.   One common format for technology training is teacher skill development that focuses on teaching specific information such as assessment techniques, discipline or child management tactics, the process of consultation, or a combination. Individual case consultation may occur during or following such technology training. It is useful to conceptualize technology training as a *continuum* within the range of consultation services that might be provided. Early reviews of the teacher training literature (e.g., Anderson & Kratochwill, 1988) suggested that a variety of formats were used including didactic instruction, role playing, feedback, modeling, and combinations thereof. Considerable support exists for teaching teachers a variety of classroom intervention strategies within the context of "positive behavioral support" (Sugai & Horner, 1999).

Training a consultee during the process of consultation, whether as the primary or ancillary focus, has some specific advantages (Kratochwill et al., 1992) that can be illustrated in research (e.g., Anderson, Kratochwill, & Bergan, 1986; Cleven & Gutkin, 1988). Anderson et al. (1986) evaluated the relative effectiveness of two teacher training packages on two consultation analogue dependent measures. The two conditions were: training in classroom behavior management tactics, consultation verbal processes, and training in consultation service delivery procedures compared to a general multidisciplinary team process conceptualized as a control condition. Teacher consultees were evaluated on their knowledge of behavioral principles and concepts as well as the frequency of specific categories of verbal behaviors during the consultation process. The behavior management and consultation training package was effective in increasing both teacher knowledge of management procedures and the frequency of teacher verbalizations regarding overt child behaviors, observation techniques, and intervention plans during the first two phases of consultation.

Cleven and Gutkin (1988) implemented a training procedure to increase teachers' understanding and use of problem definition skills during consultation interactions. Teachers who were exposed to consultation scenarios that included cognitive modeling wrote better problem definitions and were better able to describe the process for defining children's problems than those in a condition in which consultation was presented without cognitive modeling, or a control condition. The cognitive modeling group was better in their performance than the control condition.

The training implications of this area of research are clear: teacher technology training can be focused on teaching consultants to empower teachers by providing them greater skills in collaboration during the consultation process (Rosenfield, 1987). The teacher's improved ability to write problem definitions has important implications for skill generalization to other related activities, including prereferral intervention (e.g., "building team" meetings in which vague explanations and/or written descriptions on referral sheets can preclude effective brainstorming by other staff members and subsequent intervention). Whether such approaches are more effective than nonteacher training procedures remains to be determined.

Parent technology training.   As a parallel to teacher technology training, the consultant has the option of consulting with parents who have been trained in various intervention strategies to work with their child-client. A rather large literature has developed in the area of parent training that incorporates the indirect service delivery approach and might be linked to a consultation process (see, e.g., Sheridan & Kratochwill, 1992). Although it is beyond the scope of this article to review the issues pertaining to the range and scope of available parent training research that is relevant for consultation (see Briesmeister & Schaefer, 1998), there are a number of issues that have evolved from the parent training literature that have an important impact on the process and should influence the efficacy of consultation outcomes. First, such factors as low socio-economic status (SES), poor parental adjustment, inaccurate parental perceptions of child behavior, "insularity" in social relationships, and the presence of punitive and inconsistent fathering behavior have been linked to failure to parent training activities (e.g., Kramer, 1990). Single parent families have consistently been found difficult to keep in parent training (e.g., Blechman, 1984). The higher drop out rate and reduced effectiveness of standard parent training procedures when used with families with the highest need for such services warrants further research and development of technology that more appropriately matches the needs of these families.

Second, a number of parent training technologies seem useful to integrate within the field of school consultation. For example, self-help manuals or self-administered instructional materials might be used in training parents during the process of consultation. Although there is little empirical support for this kind of technology application, such a procedure might supplement more traditional case consultation (e.g., Gmeinder & Kratochwill, 1998; Webster-Stratton, 1996). Similarly, short-term workshops and didactic parent training alone, might be used to compliment individual case consultation. Although little work supports the efficacy of short-term workshops and didactic training, when combined with more conventional consultation, such approaches may be effective.

As an illustration of the integration of technology training activities and case consultation, parents might also participate in instruction that is incorporated during the process of consultation (Bergan & Kratochwill, 1990). For example, Rotto and Kratochwill (1994) demonstrated that parents can be taught such skills as instruction giving, differential attention, and time-out to effectively manage clinically significant levels of noncompliant behavior in children through the process of behavioral consultation. Such an integration of traditional case consultation with parent technology training provides a rich source of opportunities for consultation in the school psychology research. Further extensions of consultation can also be conceptualized, such as utilizing parents who are trained in treatment techniques to assist in teaching and modeling the skills to other parents (i.e., within a school-based consultation program). Unfortunately, this research has routinely, with few exceptions (e.g., Cobb & Medway, 1978), been eliminated from reviews of the consultation literature. One of the primary reasons that this literature is not featured is that it is not conceptualized as part of "consultation."

Organizational Consultation

Organizational level or system-based consultation continues to gain attention (see Senge et al., 2000) and state and federal emphasis on such efforts (see, e.g., Indiana Department of Education P.L.146–1999, P.L.193–1999, and P.L.221–1999 or http://ideanet.doe.state.in.us/pl221/statute.html). Again, in the mental health consultation literature this focus of consultation is referred to as "consultee-centered administrative consultation" and is considered among the most demanding forms of services (Caplan & Caplan, 1993). Our educational systems are inherently structured in such a way that they tend to stratify and fragment faculty, students, administrators, and staff. Stratification occurs as a natural result of separating students by year in school, by needs and proficiencies, physical location of classrooms, school board members, offsite administrators, parents, and so forth. As a result, school systems are very complex organizations with many inherent barriers to change. This complexity helps to explain why this form of consultation is so inherently demanding. Although many advocate cooperative learning for children, the idea of cooperative learning for teachers, administrators, and staff has only recently been explored (O'Neil, 1995). Organizational level consultation can focus on creating learning communities by fostering the natural relationships between children, parents, teachers, and their school. Building these relationships shifts the focus from ways of restructuring and organizing to ideals and relationships (see Wald & Castleberry, 2000).

Senge et al. (2000) emphasized the importance of shifting attention away from restructuring schools to creating the "learning community" in which everyone in the system is involved in expressing their aspirations, building awareness, and developing capabilities. The key premise behind an organizational consulting orientation lies in leveraging the significant "difference between individual capability and collective capability and individual learning and collective learning" (see O'Neil, 1995).

Wald and Castleberry (2000) discussed three assumptions regarding the learning community that illuminate how an organizational consulting approach focuses on school culture rather than structure. These assumptions include a common philosophy that bonds the community, a web of diverse relationships within the community, and a context for the emergence of unpredictable potential provided by the community. The framework Senge and his associates (2000) proposed to achieve such a learning community utilizes the five learning disciplines of personal mastery, shared vision, mental models, team learning, and systems thinking. In contrast to technology training consultation, the five disciplines are ongoing bodies of study and practice that people adopt as individuals and groups. Practicing these disciplines results in greater outcomes through the collective efforts of the individuals in the system or community.

There are several important issues that may be considered in system-based consulting that have important implications for training. The concepts underlying learning communities intuitively make sense to members of the system. Successful consultancy involves sharing the body of knowledge, facilitating the learning process of the consultees in familiarizing themselves with the body of knowledge (reading, reflecting, and discussing), coaching and mentoring, and continual follow up to sustain the momentum gained. As such, the consultant often works with a system on an ongoing basis continually tailoring material to fit system needs. The objective is to help the community members learn and create a culture that is constructive and self-sustaining and to provide school leadership with a framework to sustain this culture through, for example, school reform and development of positive behavioral support system interventions (see, e.g., Sugai & Horner, 1999).

The extraordinary complexity of school systems has been magnified with the increase in school age population and increased demands placed on school systems for nonacademic services. Because it is difficult for consultees to find time in their busy schedules to commit to see measurable results, organizational consulting is often slow to get started, but builds momentum. The momentum gained is derived from the process of fulfilling the personal visions and aspirations of the members of the learning community. Strengthening the communication and relationship between members of the learning community provides constituents with a pathway to achieving desired outcomes. Most successful outcomes grow out of multiple constituencies working together (O'Neil, 1995). Consultants must, therefore, be exposed to the literature on school reform and system change.

CORE CHARACTERISTICS OF CONSULTATION: IMPLICATIONS FOR PROFESSIONAL TRAINING

Although authors in the school consultation field feature indirect service as the primary defining characteristic, a number of other "core" features can be identified as relevant to professional training. Gutkin and Curtis (1999) reviewed some of the prominent core consultation characteristics in addition to the indirect service delivery component that serve as a blueprint for defining theory, research, and practice within school consultation. Table 2 presents these characteristics and a brief definition based on previous work. Although these characteristics may be more based on myth than data (see Witt, 1991 for this perspective), and are not always well conceptualized (Kratochwill, 1991), each category represents an important dimension that can guide a professional training curriculum within the context of the framework for problem-solving consultation. Each of these issues is now presented so that readers can consider (or reconsider) their focus within the context of the range and scope of problem solving.

Indirect Versus Direct Client Services

Consultation has historically been defined as a problem-solving process between a professional and one or more consultees who provide professional services to the client (Gutkin & Curtis, 1999; Medway, 1979). Indirect service to the client has been the primary identifying characteristic of consultation research, theory, and practice, as this definition implies. Nevertheless, this feature should be evaluated within the context of services being on a continuum of direct and indirect interventions, as in consultation and therapy (Bergan & Kratochwill, 1990). A consultant may, in fact, provide some direct services to the client at various stages during the consultation process (see Piersel & Kratochwill, 1979 for an early example). An "either/or" orientation to service delivery further militates against the possibility of high quality services that might be delivered when direct intervention is necessary. In addition, direct intervention with a client may be needed in cases where it is impossible for the consultee to implement treatment due to lack of skill, time, or other factors that limit mediator-based services. The point is that the consultant should become involved in treating the client when there is a compelling professional opportunity for direct services or when ethical and legal mandates suggest this focus is the most effective way to deliver treatment services.

Aside from these issues, a high priority in training is to match evidence-based treatments to the type a mediator-based service approach. Some evidence-based treatments such as parent training (see Webster-Stratton, 1996) should be considered in practice because they match an indirect service model. In other cases, the treatment might be better offered through direct services or a combination of direct and indirect approaches such as in flooding treatment of posttraumatic stress disorder. These issues represent a high priority in our graduate training programs and have been recently elaborated in the literature (see Kratochwill & Stoiber, 2000; Stoiber & Kratochwill, 2000).

TABLE 2
Core Characteristics of School-based Consultation Services with Implications for Graduate Training

Characteristic	Traditional Training Assumption	Revised Training Assumption
Service delivery format	Treatment is delivered through a consultee (e.g., parent or teacher) rather than directly through the psychologist	Treatment is delivered through direct and indirect contact with the client
Consultation focus	Provision of services to clients	Provision of services to client and/or consultee
Goals of consultation	Remediation and/or prevention process goals: skill development	Remediation and/or prevention process goal: skill development
Consultant-consultee relationship	Meaningful collaborative relationship characterized by openness and trust	Collaboration ranges from maximum to minimum depending on the knowledge and skills of the consultee
Coordinate power status	A coordinate power status is vital. A hierarchical relationship may militate against good communication and rapport	Power status can range from coordinate to hierarchical depending on the status of the consulte
Right to reject consultant suggestions	The consultee has the right to reject the consultant's suggestions	The consultee may or may not be able to reject the consultant's suggestions depending on the negotiated relationship
Consultee involvement	The consultee should be actively involved in the consultation process	The consultee should be actively involved in the consultation process and may share treatment responsibilities with the consultant
Voluntary participation	The consultation relationship is initiated voluntarily by the consultee	Voluntary participation is ideal but may be impossible with some consultant-consultee relationships
Confidentiality	Confidentiality of consultee–consultant communication is essential in successful consultation	Confidentiality may not be possible with some consultees such as children

Consultant–Consultee Relationship/Coordinate Power Status

The issues pertaining to the consultant–consultee relationship remain a prominent concern across all the alternative frameworks for consultation services reviewed previously. However, graduate training programs will need to reconceptualize the issues pertaining to relationship variables depending on the mode of problem-solving consultation service delivery practiced. As an obvious example, child consultee relationship issues within a child consultee context will be very different than those pertaining to adult mediated intervention programs.

A traditional assumption of consultation approaches has been that the relationship is collaborative and that consultants and consultees have equivalent authority in the decision-making process in the delivery of intervention services. Some research has indicated that consultees (e.g., teachers) may prefer collaborative relationships in the consultation process (e.g., Babcock & Pryzwansky, 1983; Pryzwansky & White, 1983). Whether a collaborative approach in consultation is empirically supportable, however, remains to be determined. This assumption may need further empirical test and as Witt (1991) argued, some research suggests that a noncollaborative hierarchical relationship actually occurs in some consultation models (e.g., Erchul, 1987). Moreover, there are at least two issues to be considered with regard to coordinate power status. First, there is the issue of the effectiveness of consultation under conditions of coordinate power. Second, there is the issue of whether consultation relationships in practice are truly collaborative. Both issues are in need of research attention.

Our broadened conceptual framework presented previously would further support the need for research on this construct since the nature of collaboration may vary across different consultee foci and skill levels. A useful distinction may be the option that consultants can be both directive and collaborative (Gutkin & Curtis, 1999). Consultation between a special education teacher who has extensive training in classroom interventions and a school psychologist may be a much more collaborative and non-hierarchical relationship than consultation with a novice general education teacher. Even more compelling, a more directive relationship is likely in cases where the professional is consulting with parents, and certainly in the case where the child serves as the consultee.

Relatedly, the nature of discourse may differ depending on the type of consultee (Gutkin & Curtis, 1999). Some limited work related to "influence tactics" (as it is referred to in the counseling literature) has been done within a consultative framework (e.g., Witt, 1991); that is, the consultant may use different patterns of dialogue depending on the type (parent, teacher, etc.), role (coordinate status, subordinate status), gender, and so forth, of the consultee. Further examination of such variables may help to illuminate the nature of collaboration. What does appear to be needed in these areas is a careful definition of the construct of collaboration across the different service dimensions presented here.

Consultees Right to Reject Consultant Suggestions

Voluntary participation (also discussed following as an ethical issue) in consultation is deemed important and has represented the hallmark of consultation professional practice across the types of consultation presented in this article. However, voluntary participation could result in the consultee "saying one thing and doing another." For example, the consultee may not carry out the treatment program with integrity even after making a verbal commitment to do so (Wickstrom, Jones, LaFleur, & Witt, 1998). It is logical to assume that as one deviates from the coordinate power relationship between the consultant and consultee the issue of "rejection" of treatment may need to be reconceptualized. Certainly it is the *right* of the consultee to reject the consultant's suggestions.

The issue of following the consultant's recommendations may also be framed within the literature on resistance and acceptability of interventions. In the former area considerable research has been developing in the area of parent-mediated interventions and strategies to overcome such resistance (e.g., Chamberlain & Baldwin, 1988). The findings from this work have been recommended for consideration in consultation where the primary focus is a teacher (Witt, 1990). Resistance is analyzed in the context of an assessment technology to identify it and strategies to overcome it during the process of consultation. Clearly the future research agenda in school psychology must be incorporating the research base from parent technology training in case centered consultation with teachers and parents, and possibly, children.

In the case of evaluation of interventions, a growing body of research suggests the importance of treatment acceptability (e.g., Elliott, 1988; Reimers, Wacker, & Koeppel, 1987). However, most of the empirical work in treatment acceptability has occurred with teachers and to some extent with parents, and much of the research is analogue in nature. In the context of this discussion, acceptability has an obvious relation to the issue of rejection of consultants' treatment suggestions. Furthermore, researchers must evaluate children's acceptability of interventions and how they perceive child-mediated interventions implemented with peers. Moreover, the issue of adult acceptability of children implementing interventions with them has been virtually unexplored in the treatment acceptability literature. We do not know how adults will act when various types of child interventions are implemented or even if adults will perceive child-based interventions as acceptable, regardless of the content. These issues are obviously a priority in training within the context of a broader framework of consultation service delivery.

Involvement of the Consultee in the Consultation Process

The consultee's involvement in consultation has been seen as critical to the success of positive client outcomes (Gutkin & Curtis, 1999). High levels of consultee involvement should be positive for consultation outcomes, but how much active participation occurs and the variables related to involvement is unclear. The level of involvement of the consultee within our broadened framework can be conceptualized as a variable that is affected by the particular type of consultation. This raises some issues that will need to be addressed in professional training. First, involvement in the process can be conceptualized in terms of *who* is serving as the consultee. In some cases, multiple consultees might be involved such as in technology training applications or organizational consultation where groups and the system are the focus of consultation efforts. Thus, in conceptualizing involvement, a new range of variables may occur beyond the single consultee as the primary focus of implementing consultation services.

Second, the type of consultation relationship may have a bearing on the level of involvement. Although we know of no empirical data suggesting that relationship variables are salient, from our own experience, teachers, for example, appear to be more willing participants in the consultation process in conjoint activities when parents are present. It is unclear whether the parents' presence "motivates" the teacher, but it likely sets the occasion for more significant involvement because of established historical practice.

Third, the consultee's "involvement" in the consultation process, whatever their relationship to the problem and the consultant, may be an issue of treatment integrity. That is, the consultee's commitment to be involved in the process might need to be conceptualized as a target for direct intervention by the consultant. Fortunately, the importance of treatment integrity within the consultation field has received greater attention in professional training and research in recent years (e.g., Gresham, 1989). Of interest, few researchers prior to 1987 actually incorporated this feature within the methodology (see Gresham & Kendall, 1987). Treatment integrity may be a more salient concern than traditional conceptualizations of interpersonal skills in dealing with the involvement of the consultee in the consultation process. With a broad conceptual framework for how consultation might be implemented, the targets of treatment integrity may vary across various consultant–consultee combinations. Some research questions are as follows: How can we insure integrity across various consultees? Do strategies to promote treatment integrity vary from teacher-to-parent-to-child consultees? Are there other mediating variables that influence involvement? Does level of training (such as in technology training) promote more involvement than those formats that do not incorporate a formal training process in consultation? These are among some of the salient issues that need to be addressed in the future research. They need to be taken into account in professional training.

Ethical Issues

Clearly, voluntary participation of consultee and client is good ethical practice in consultation (Hughes, 1986). Beyond this ethical issue, voluntary composition of the consultation relationship may promote a higher level of participation and treatment integrity. Nevertheless, the broadened conceptual framework for consultation services and training that we have previously presented raises some issues about the voluntary nature of consultation that extend beyond the usual case-centered consultee issues. For example, involvement of children in the process of working with their peers has raised some issues in the peer tutoring literature (e.g., benefits derived for the tutor and tutee, nature and type of peer training). Just as a consultant cannot "force" a teacher to serve as a consultee, the consultant cannot force a child to serve as a mediator to implement an intervention with an adult or with his or her peers.

The issues pertaining to confidentiality and related legal and ethical issues have been discussed in the consultation literature (e.g., Hughes, 1986). Although we will not review this discussion in detail here, the involvement of parents in the consultation process raises new issues in legal and ethical domains that may need to be resolved. For example, the degree to which the consultant accepts responsibility for his/her recommendations and for the child's well-being may differ than in a situation where both parties are employees of the same school district.

Involvement of the child as the mediator with adults raises some interesting issues in the field that have not been addressed in great detail. For example, in the case of implementing an intervention through a child mediator, how much information should be provided to the adult regarding what will be done. The consultant needs to be aware of the special relationship issues that occur in working with children and empowering them to develop intervention programs that influence their environment. In general, a consultant should be competent in his/her ability to assess a child's developmental level and individual maturity before making decisions about the level of responsibility to present to the child.

Special issues can also be raised with respect to the child's involvement with peers such as in peer tutoring interventions, or when the child serves as a reinforcing and/or assessment agent for his or her peers (Topping & Ehly, 2001). What safeguards should be developed with child interventions that are indirect? What ethical and legal responsibility does the consultant have in these services as, for example, ensuring confidentiality when a child is serving in the role of consultee? These are some issues that will need to be addressed at both the conceptual and perhaps the empirical level.

Organizational consultation raises issues as well. The sharing of information is of special concern in organizational consulting because the "client" is defined broadly. For example, it could refer to the school administration, a problem solving team of professionals, or a group of teachers at a certain grade level. Thus, the usual parameters of confidentiality may not be the same as when a consultant works with a consultee to serve a child client. One important question that needs to be addressed is whether the school or system is ready to involve all constituents in the learning community in the consultation process. Most traditional school systems have limited experience with this level of openness and direct involvement, particularly when it comes to participation in what traditionally has been considered administrative responsibilities. In addition, such issues as "voluntary participation" in consultation services can be challenged when system change is mandated by the school administration.

CONCLUDING PERSPECTIVES

Given that indirect or mediator-based service delivery becomes the primary defining characteristic of consultation, several new domains of practice can become new foci of future training for a variety of professions involved in school problem-solving consultation services. In some cases, considerable theory development and research have occurred (e.g., with parents) and in some cases research is in its infancy (e.g., child-based). It is unclear what options for practice will occur within the field. It is clear that research in the areas outlined in this article can further the range and scope of consultation training in our preservice graduate programs and in inservice training of school-based professionals.

ACKNOWLEDGMENTS

The writing efforts in this article were supported, in part, through grants to the first author from the United States Department of Education, Office of Special Education and Rehabilitation Services, and by the Wisconsin Center for Education Research, School of Education, University of Wisconsin-Madison. The opinions expressed in this publication are those of the authors and do not necessarily reflect the views of the U.S. Department of Education or the Wisconsin Center for Education Research.

An earlier version of this manuscript was developed by the first author during a graduate course at the University of Wisconsin-Madison taught by the first author. The first author expresses appreciation to Todd Gorges, Todd Liolios, Pamela Loitz, Sara K. Ousdigian, Michele M. Plunge, Laural A. Sabin, and Melissa Twernbold for their input into the article.

We thank Karen O'Connell and Lois Triemstra for their assistance with the manuscript.

REFERENCES

Anderson, T. K., & Kratochwill, T. R. (1988). Dissemination of behavioral procedures in the schools: Issues in training. In J. C. Witt, S. N. Elliott, & F. M. Gresham (Eds.), *Handbook of behavior therapy in education* (pp. 217–244). New York: Plenum.

Anderson, T. K., Kratochwill, T. R., & Bergan, J. R. (1986). Training teachers in behavioral consultation and therapy: An analysis of verbal behaviors. *Journal of School Psychology, 24*, 229–241.

Axelrod, S., Hall, R. V., & Maxwell, A. (1972). Use of peer attention to increase study behavior. *Behavior Therapy, 3*, 349–351.

Babcock, N. L., & Pryzwansky, W. B. (1983). Models of consultation: Preferences of educational professionals at five stages of service. *Journal of School Psychology, 21*, 359–366.

Bell, R. Q., & Harper, L. V. (1977). *Child effects on adults.* Hillsdale, NJ: Lawrence Erlbaum Associates, Inc.

Bergan, J. R. (1977). *Behavioral consultation.* Columbus, OH: Charles E. Merrill.

Bergan, J. R., & Kratochwill, T. R. (1990). *Behavioral consultation in applied settings*. New York: Plenum.

Blechman, E. A. (1984). Competent parents, competent children: Behavioral objectives of parent training. In R. F. Dangel & R. A. Polster (Eds.), *Parent training: Foundations of research and practice* (pp. 34–66). New York: Guilford.

Briesmeister, J. M., & Schaefer, C. E. (Eds.). (1998). *Handbook of parent training* (2nd ed.). New York: Wiley.

Caplan, G., & Caplan, R. B. (1993). *Mental health consultation and collaboration*. San Francisco: Jossey-Bass.

Carr, E. G., Taylor, J. C., & Robinson, S. (1991). The effects of severe behavior problems in children on the teaching behavior of adults. *Journal of Applied Behavior Analysis, 24*, 523–535.

Chamberlain, P., & Baldwin, D. V. (1988). Client resistance to parent training: Its therapeutic measurement. In T. R. Kratochwill (Ed.), *Advances in School Psychology VI* (pp. 131–171). Hillsdale, NJ: Lawrence Erlbaum Associates, Inc.

Cleven, C. A., & Gutkin, T. B. (1988). Cognitive modeling of consultation processes: A means for improving consultee's problem definition skills. *Journal of School Psychology, 26*, 379–389.

Cobb, D. E., & Medway, F. J. (1978). Determinants of effectiveness in parent consultation. *Journal of Community Psychology, 6*, 229–240.

Conoley, J. C., & Gutkin, T. B. (1986). School psychology: A reconceptualization of service delivery realities. In S. N. Elliott & J. C. Witt (Eds.), *The delivery of psychological services in schools: Concepts, processes, and issues* (pp. 393–424). Hillsdale, NJ: Lawrence Erlbaum Associates, Inc.

Elliott, S. N. (1988). Acceptability of behavioral treatments: Review of variables that influence treatment selection. *Professional Psychology: Research and Practice, 19*, 68–80.

Emery, R. E., Binkoff, J. A., Houts, A. C., & Carr, E. G. (1983). Children as independent variables: Some clinical implications of child effects. *Behavior Therapy, 14*, 398–412.

Erchul, W. P. (1987). A relational communication analysis of control in school consultation. *Professional School Psychology, 2*, 113–124.

Frisby, C. L. (1998). Formal communication within school psychology: A 1990–1994 journal citation analyses. *School Psychology Review, 27*, 304–316.

Fuchs, D., Fuchs, L. S., Dulan, J., Roberts, H., & Fernstrom, P. (1992). Where is the research on consultative effectiveness? *Journal of Educational and Psychological Consultation, 3*, 151–174.

Gmeinder, K., & Kratochwill, T. R. (1998). Short-term, home-based intervention for child noncompliance using behavioral consultation and a self-help manual. *Journal of Educational and Psychological Consultation, 9*, 91–117.

Graubard, P. S., Rosenberg, H., & Miller, M. B. (1971). Student applications of behavior modification to teachers and environments or ecological approaches to social deviancy. In E. A. Ramp & B. L. Hopkins (Eds.), *A new direction for education: Behavior analysis*. Lawrence, KS: The University of Kansas Support and Development Center for Follow Through.

Gresham, F. M. (1989). Assessment of treatment integrity in school consultation and prereferral intervention. *School Psychology Review, 18*, 37–50.

Gresham, F. M., & Kendall, G. K. (1987). School consultation research: Methodological critique and future research directions. *School Psychology Review, 16*, 306–316.

Gutkin, T. B., & Curtis, M. J. (1999). School-based consultation theory and practice: The art and science of indirect service delivery. In C. R. Reynolds & T. B. Gutkin (Eds.), *The handbook of school psychology* (3rd ed.). New York: Wiley.

Hetherington, E. M., & Parke, R. D. (1986). *Child psychology* (3rd ed.). New York: McGraw-Hill.

Hughes, J. N. (1986). Ethical issues in school consultation. *School Psychology Review, 15,* 489–499.

Ikeda, M. J., Tilly, W. D., Stumme, J., Volmer, L., & Allison, R. (1996). Agency-wide implementation of problem solving consultation: Foundation and current implementation, and future directions. *School Psychology Quarterly, 11,* 228–243.

Kalfus, G. R. (1984). Peer mediated intervention: A critical review. *Child and Family Behavior Therapy, 6,* 17–43.

Kazdin, A. E. (1988). *Child psychotherapy: Developing and identifying effective treatments.* New York: Pergamon.

Kramer, J. J. (1990). Training parents as behavior change agents: Successes, failures, and suggestions for school psychologists. In T. B. Gutkin & C. R. Reynolds (Eds.), *Handbook of school psychology* (2nd ed., pp. 685–702). New York: Wiley.

Kratochwill, T. R. (1991). Defining constructs in consultation research: An important agenda in the 1990s. *Journal of Educational and Psychological Consultation, 2,* 291–294.

Kratochwill, T. R., & Bergan, J. R. (1990). *Behavioral consultation in applied settings.* New York: Plenum.

Kratochwill, T. R., Bergan, J. R., Sheridan, S. M., & Elliott, S. N. (1998). Assumptions of behavioral consultation: After all is said and done more has been done than said. *School Psychology Quarterly, 13,* 63–80.

Kratochwill, T. R., Elliott, S. N., & Busse, R. T. (1995). Behavioral consultation: A five-year evaluation of consultant and client outcomes. *School Psychology Quarterly, 10,* 87–117.

Kratochwill, T. R., Elliott, S. N., & Callan-Stoiber, K. (2002). *Best practices in school-based problem-solving consultation.* In A. Thomas and J. Grimes (Eds.), Best practices in school psychology IV. Bethesda, MD: The National Association of School Psychologists.

Kratochwill, T. R., Elliott, S. N., & Stoiber, K. C. (2002). Best practices in school-based problem-solving consultation. In A. Thomas & T. Grimes (Eds.), *Best practices in school psychology* (Vol. IV). Washington, DC: National Association of School Psychologists.

Kratochwill, T. R., Sladeczek, I., & Plunge, M. (1995). The evolution of behavior consultation. *Journal of Educational and Psychological Consultation, 6,* 145–157.

Kratochwill, T. R., Sheridan, S. M., Carrington-Rotto, P., & Salmon, D. (1992). Preparation of school psychologists in behavioral consultation service delivery. In T. R. Kratochwill, S. N. Elliott, & M. Gettinger (Eds.), *Advances in school psychology* (Vol. III, pp. 115–152). Hillsdale, NJ: Lawrence Erlbaum Associates, Inc.

Kratochwill, T. R., Sheridan, S. M., & VanSomeren, K. R. (1988). Research in behavioral consultation: Current status and future directions. In F. West (Ed.), *School consultation: Interdisciplinary perspectives on theory, research, training, and practice* (pp. 77–104). Austin, TX: University of Texas Press.

Kratochwill, T. R., & Stoiber, K. C. (2000). Empirically supported interventions and school psychology: Conceptual and practice issues – Part II. *School Psychology Quarterly, 15,* 233–253.

Lepage, K., Kratochwill, T. R., & Elliott, S. N. (2001). *Competency based consultation training: An evaluation of consultant outcomes, treatment effects, and consumer satisfaction.* Manuscript submitted for publication.

Lovitt, T. C., Lovitt, A. O., Eaton, M. D., & Kirkwood, M. (1973). The deceleration of inappropriate comments by a natural consequence. *Journal of School Psychology, 11,* 148–156.

McKenzie, M. L., & Budd, K. S. (1981). A peer tutoring package to increase mathematics performance: Examination of generalized changes in classroom behavior. *Education and Treatment of Children, 4,* 1–15.

Medway, F. J. (1979). How effective is school consultation: A review of recent research. *Journal of School Psychology, 17,* 275–282.

Noell, G. H., Gresham, F. M., & Duhon, G. (1998). Fundamental agreements and epistemological differences in differentiating what was said from what was done in behavioral consultation. *School Psychology Quarterly, 13,* 81–88.

Noell, G. H., & Witt, J. C. (1996). A critical re-evaluation of five fundamental assumptions underlying behavioral consultation. *School Psychology Quarterly, 11,* 189–203.

Ollendick, T. H., & Cerny, J. A. (1981). *Clinical behavior therapy with children.* New York: Plenum.

O'Neil, J. (1995). On schools as learning organizations: A conversation with Peter Senge. *Educational Leadership, 52,* 20–23.

Piersel, W. C., & Kratochwill, T. R. (1979). Self-observation and behavior change: Applications to academic and adjustment problems through behavioral consultation. *Journal of School Psychology, 17,* 151–161.

Pryzwansky, W. B., & White, G. W. (1983). The influence of consultee characteristics on preferences for consultation approaches. *Professional Psychology: Research and Practice, 14,* 457–461.

Ramirez, S., Lepage, K. M., Kratochwill, T. R., & Duffy, J. (1998). Multicultural issues in school-based consultation: Conceptual and research considerations. *Journal of School Psychology, 36,* 479–509.

Reimers, T. M., Wacker, D. P., & Koeppel, G. (1987). Acceptability of behavioral treatments: A review of the literature. *School Psychology Review, 16,* 212–227.

Rhoades, M. M., & Kratochwill, T. R. (1998). Parent training and consultation: An analysis of a homework intervention program. *School Psychology Quarterly, 13,* 241–264.

Roberts, M. C., Erickson, M. T., LaGreca, A. M., Russ, S. W., Vargas, L. A., Carlson, C. I., et al. (1998). A model of training psychologists to provide services for children and adolescents. *Professional Psychology: Research and Practice, 29,* 293–299.

Rosenfield, S. A. (1987). *Instructional consultation.* Hillsdale, NJ: Lawrence Erlbaum Associates, Inc.

Rotto, P. C., & Kratochwill, T. R. (1994). Behavioral consultation with parents: Using competency-based training to modify child noncompliance. *School Psychology Review, 23,* 669–693.

Schulberg, H. C., & Jerrell, J. M. (1983). Consultation. In M. Hersen, A. E. Kazdin, & A. S. Bellack (Eds.), *The clinical psychology handbook* (pp. 783–798). New York: Pergamon.

Senge, P., Cambron-McCabe, N., Lucas, T., Smith, B., Dutton, J., & Kleiner, A. (2000). *Schools that learn.* New York: Doubleday.

Sheridan, S. M. (1992). What do we mean when we say "collaboration?" *Journal of Educational and Psychological Consultation, 3,* 89–92.

Sheridan, S. M. (2000). Considerations of multiculturalism and diversity in behavioral consultation with parents and teachers. *School Psychology Review, 29,* 344–353.

Sheridan, S. M. & Kratochwill, T. R. (1992). Behavioral parent/teacher consultation: Conceptual and research considerations. *Journal of School Psychology, 30,* 117–139.

Sheridan, S. M., Kratochwill, T. R., & Bergan, J. R. (1996). *Conjoint behavioral consultation: A procedural guide.* New York: Plenum.

Sheridan, S. M., Kratochwill, T. R., & Elliott, S. N. (1990). Behavioral consultation with parents and teachers: Delivering treatment for socially withdrawn children at home and school. *School Psychology Review, 19,* 33–52.

Stewart, K. J. (1986). Innovative practice of indirect service delivery: Realities and idealities. *School Psychology Review, 15,* 466–478.

Stoiber, K. C., & Kratochwill, T. R. (2000). Empirically supported interventions and school psychology: Rationale and methodological issues – Part I. *School Psychology Quarterly, 15,* 75–105.

Sugai, G., & Horner, R. (1999). Discipline and behavioral support: Practices, pitfalls, and promises. *Effective School Practices, 17,* 10–17.

Tharp, R. G., & Wetzel, R. J. (1969). *Behavioral modification in the natural environment.* New York: Academic.

Topping, K. J., & Ehly, S. W. (2001). Peer assisted learning: A framework for consultation. *Journal of Educational and Psychological Consultation, 12,* 113–132.

Vernberg, E. M., & Reppucci, N. D. (1986). Behavioral consultation. In F. V. Mannino, E. J. Trickett, M. F. Shore, M. G. Kidder, & G. Levin (Eds.), *Handbook of mental health consultation* (pp. 49–80). Rockville, MD: National Institute of Mental Health.

Wald, P. J., & Castleberry, M. S., (2000). *Educators as learners: Creating a professional learning community in your school.* Alexandria, VA: Association for Supervision and Curriculum Development.

Watson, T. S., & Robinson, S. L. (1996). Direct behavioral consultation: An alternative to traditional behavioral consultation. *School Psychology Quarterly, 11,* 267–278.

Watson, T. S., Sterling, H. E., & McDade, A. (1997). Demythifying behavioral consultation. *School Psychology Review, 26,* 467–474.

Webster-Stratton, C. H. (1996). Early intervention with videotape modeling: Programs for families of children with oppositional defiant disorder or conduct disorder. In E. D. Hibbs & P. S. Jensen (Eds.), *Psychosocial treatments for child and adolescent disorders: Empirically based strategies for clinical practice* (pp. 435–474). Washington, DC: American Psychological Association.

Wickstrom, K. F., Jones, K. M., LaFleur, L. H., & Witt, J. C. (1998). An analysis of treatment integrity in school-based behavioral consultation. *School Psychology Quarterly, 13,* 141–154.

Witt, J. C. (1991). Collaboration in school-based consultation: Myth in need of data. *Journal of Educational and Psychology Consultation, 1,* 367–370.

Witt, J. C. (1990). Face-to-face verbal interactions in school-based consultation: A review of the literature. *School Psychology Quarterly, 5,* 199–210.

Thomas R. Kratochwill received his PhD from the University of Wisconsin-Madison in 1973 with a specialization in School Psychology. He joined the faculty at the University of Arizona in 1973 in the Department of Educational Psychology, School Psychology Program serving as Coordinator of the Office of Child Research. In 1983 he returned to the University of Wisconsin-Madison. Currently, he is Co-Director of Child Adolescent Mental Health and Education Information Resource Center at the University of Wisconsin-Madison.

Paul H. Pittman is an Associate Professor of Operations Management at Indiana University Southeast and earned his PhD in Production and Operation Management at the University of Georgia. He is Certified in Production and Inventory Management at the fellow level through APICS, The Educational Society for Resource Management., and is a certified Jonah with the A.Y. Goldratt Institute in the Theory of Constraints. Paul is the principle partner of The Lamp Group with over 10 years of experience assisting variety of organizations including schools in learning and applying the concepts of organizational learning, systems thinking, quality, project management, and constraints management.

JOURNAL OF EDUCATIONAL AND PSYCHOLOGICAL CONSULTATION, 13(1&2), 97–111
Copyright © 2002, Lawrence Erlbaum Associates, Inc.

Developing Instructional Consultants: From Novice to Competent to Expert

Sylvia Rosenfield
University of Maryland

The development of instructional consultants requires both an understanding of the essential elements of instructional consultation (IC) and a conceptual model for development of skills. IC is a collaborative stage-based process that focuses on academic and behavioral concerns from an ecological perspective. It also emphasizes the importance of language and working relationships in the consultation process. In the first level of development, novice consultants develop awareness and conceptual understanding, as well as limited skills. Competency is achieved through application of skills in school settings with supervision that focuses, with the assistance of audiotaping the consultation sessions, on language and relationship issues as well as content. Advanced skills and proficiency emerge during extended opportunity for practice, supervision and research among those individuals who become interested in developing expertise in this domain of practice. Most training programs provide limited opportunities for competency and expertise to be developed past the novice level. It is essential to enhance educational opportunities and options if consultation practice is to achieve its full potential.

Teaching consultation for nearly three decades has been a major focus of my professional life. A review of past syllabi, from the first offering of the course at Fordham University in the early 1970's to my current two-semester course at the University of Maryland (current syllabi are available on re-

Correspondence should be addressed to Sylvia Rosenfield, Department of Counseling and Personnel Services, University of Maryland, College Park, MD 20742. E-mail: sr47@umail.umd.edu

quest from the author) revealed considerable overlap over time, at least in the first consultation course. However, my perspective on what is required to develop true expertise in consultation practice has evolved over the years.

To examine this perspective on the development of consultation expertise, I would like to briefly describe the essential elements of instructional consultation (IC; Rosenfield, 1987), the educational processes used, and finally, indicate some issues that require additional attention. The education sequence described here is addressed largely to preservice education for graduate students in school psychology, school counseling, and special education. The process of educating working professionals from multiple disciplines in IC and the IC-Team model (Rosenfield & Gravois, 1996), is described elsewhere (e.g., Gravois, Rosenfield, & Vail, 1999; Gravois, Babinski, & Knotek, this issue).

ESSENTIAL ELEMENTS OF IC

In brief, IC is a collaborative stage-based problem solving process that focuses on academic and behavioral concerns in school settings (see Rosenfield, 2002; Rosenfield, 1987, for a more complete description of IC). IC is, fundamentally, a form of consultee-centered consultation. Although the concerns presented for problem solving typically involve students, the focus is on the consultees, most typically classroom or special education teachers, who have concerns about individual students, groups of students, or teaching/classroom management practices. These concerns may involve lack of skill, lack of knowledge, lack of self-confidence or lack of objectivity, as in mental health consultation (Caplan, 1970).

Addressing such concerns requires content knowledge in areas such as classroom instructional assessment and intervention design as well as process skills. However, many content areas are developed outside of the consultation course itself, and will not be described here. For example, a school based behavioral assessment and intervention course is a prerequisite to the consultation courses that I teach. Some additional content knowledge is developed during the courses, as student consultants are expected to broaden their repertoire of empirically supported interventions as they design interventions with their consultees in the cases they are assigned. Sharing of interventions during class discussion and presentations enable other students to benefit as well.

The essential elements of IC that are developed in the courses include: (a) conduct of the stages of consultation, (b) emphasis on data-based decision making, (c) skills in working with academic concerns in school consultation, (d) focus on the language used in sessions, and (e) development of a *working* relationship.

Consultation Stages

Like other forms of consultation, especially behavioral consultation, there is a focus on problem solving stages, including contracting (obtaining informed consent to participate in the consultation process), problem identification and analysis, intervention design and implementation, monitoring of implementation, and termination. Each stage has specific tasks to be completed before moving on to the next one (see Rosenfield, 1987, 2002).

Data-Based Decision Making

Data-based decision making is an integral component of IC, as it is to behavioral consultation. Gathering systematic data on academic and behavioral concerns is an essential element of IC at multiple stages. Evaluation during intervention, even when using research-based strategies, is critical, as it is not possible to determine the effectiveness of a specific intervention in any given situation (Rosenfield, 2000b). Comparing data taken at baseline and intervention phases is essential to determine the effectiveness of the intervention or the need to change the intervention design if there is a lack of progress.

Emphasis on Academic Concerns

IC has a specific focus on academic concerns. Although behavioral as well as instructional concerns are brought to the instructional consultant, appropriate academic progress is a pervasive consideration because of its centrality to the goals of schooling and the inherent relationship in many cases between academic and behavioral concerns. Because of the ecological focus of IC, skills are required in assessing and intervening in all aspects of the instructional triangle, i.e., "the student's entry level skills, the design of instruction, and the actual task the student is asked to perform" (Rosenfield, 1995, p. 320). The focus on the learner is on alterable learner variables (Bloom, 1976), such as current behavior and academic skills, rather than stable traits such as intelligence. Skills in curriculum-based assessment (e.g., Cramer & Rosenfield, 1999; Gravois & Gickling, 2002) and functional behavior assessment are critical elements, and instructional consultants must also be able to address research based academic intervention components (e.g., Ysseldyke & Christenson, 1993) as well as more traditional behavioral interventions.

Communication Skills

Another major assumption of IC is that consultation is essentially a communication process between consultant and consultee, and the language systems approach (Rosenfield, 1999; White, Summerlin, Loos, & Epstein, 1992) provides a foundation for understanding the consultation process. The language systems approach defines the core of consultation as a linguistic event in which new meanings are co-constructed through dialogue. The consultant has major responsibility for managing the process, creating space for and facilitating the consultation conversation. Therefore, the verbal interactions that define consultation are a focus for case supervision. The language of the consultant and consultee is examined in detail and effective communication skills are developed.

Communication training also incorporates research from social psychology of what happens to communicators during the process of talking about a topic (see, e.g., Higgins, 1999). Relevant topics related to the definition of a student's referral problem on both consultant and consultee include audience tuning, shared reality, and correspondence bias (Higgins, 1999).

Audience tuning. Research on audience tuning indicates that individuals modify their message to take into account their perceptions about what another person wants to hear. This requires that consultants understand how consultees modify their message to take into account their perceptions about what they believe the consultant wants them to share. For example, when school psychologists do IC, teachers are more likely to use labels such as attention deficit disorder and learning disability in describing the problem, as they assume that most school psychologists are interested in and knowledgeable about those disorders, as opposed to classroom learning and behavior.

Shared reality.   Research has demonstrated that talking about a topic with another person generates beliefs about the objectivity of the message. Thus, the more a teacher talks about the problems of the student to a consultant, who provides active listening responses, the more likely the teacher is to see the problem as objectively real.

Correspondence bias.   Correspondence bias refers to the tendency to view the person rather than the situation as the source of behavior. When teachers have concerns about students, there is a strong bias toward seeing the student as the source of the problem rather than viewing the ecology within which the problem occurs as relevant to the problem definition.

Working Relationship

Finally, the nature of the relationship between the consultant and the consultee is an important element in IC. There is an emphasis on building a collaborative working relationship. Collaboration is valued for its contribution to building a learning community in a school (e.g., Rosenfield, 2002), or, as one teacher put it, "a networking of brains." Moreover, there is the assumption that a collaborative working relationship facilitates treatment adherence at the stage of intervention implementation (Rosenfield, 1987). However a working relationship also must provide for authenticity, that is, being able to say what one wants to say effectively and honestly, especially when there is a possibility that the consultee and consultant will not be in agreement about an issue.

A FRAMEWORK FOR EDUCATING CONSULTANTS

The development of a skilled instructional consultant is a complex process that unfolds over time. Alexander (1997) suggested that individuals develop in a given domain from acclimation to competence to expertise. In each of these stages, different activities and strategies are required to help the student develop attitudes, knowledge and skills within the domain. Paralleling the developmental process suggested by Alexander is a set of training stages in practitioner skill acquisition identified by Joyce and Showers (1980): awareness and understanding; skill acquisition; application of skills; and advanced application skill development. The consultation training model for IC builds on both the Alexander and Joyce and Showers frameworks, as delineated in Table 1.

Acclimation

A student enters the acclimation stage with little or no knowledge of the domain. Didactic activities build knowledge, which the student attempts to incorporate, but knowledge is typically fragmented at this stage (Alexander, 1997). In practice situations, novice consultants are highly dependent on external guidance. They have a set of general strategies that are often ineffectively executed. During this stage, it is essential to stress what is important to help the student separate key information, provide opportunities to explore ideas deeply that can sow the seeds of individual interest, and engage them actively in strategic processing and self-regulation (Alexander, 1997). Joyce and Showers (1980) considered this the stage of building awareness and conceptual understanding, and skill acquisition.

IC training begins with a didactic/practicum course, in which activities include lecture, discussion, and readings to build a knowledge base in the domain of consultation. Basic topics include discussion of advantages or disadvantages of indirect service delivery; models of and critical issues in consultation, including multicultural issues; and legal and ethical issues. To develop an ecological perspective, students are introduced to the concept of the school as a culture. They develop a group project that engages them in actively processing information about school culture as it applies to indirect service delivery and reflect on their participation as a member of this group.

Skill acquisition at the acclimation stage begins with awareness and conceptual understanding about the nature and purpose of the collaborative working relationship, key communication skills and the problem solving stages through readings, lectures and classroom discussion. Students are provided with checklists containing the essential tasks to be completed in each of the problem solving stages. Skill acquisition also builds on this didactic knowledge through observing consultants in the schools and on videotapes. Other critical activities include role-playing and simulations in the course sessions. In class they have the opportunity to practice skills in role-playing situations. For example, they may role-play contracting with a peer. Prior to beginning their first consultation case in the school setting, each student is videotaped on a simulation designed to elicit their skills in IC problem identification (Jones, 1999) and then view their own videotape using a manual for evaluating their skills in problem identifica-

TABLE 1
A Model for Consultant Development

Developmental Stage	Training Stage	Instructional Activities
Novice—acclimation	Awareness and understanding	Lecture, discussion, reading, observation
	Skill acquisition	Classroom simulations and role plays; videotaped simulation
Competence	Application of skills	Consultation cases, taped and supervised
Proficiency—expertise	Advanced skill development	Additional practice of consultation; continued professional development; research; supervision of others; teaching

tion (Tarakan, 1996). The stage of acclimation is generally accomplished in the first course in consultation. A take-home examination on their knowledge and skills, relying heavily on analyzing case material, occurs during the latter half of the semester.

Competence

The second stage is competence, where students consolidate subject matter knowledge around domain defining principles, and anchor their thinking around key principles. Strategic processing around routine problems becomes more automatic, and novel problems can be addressed more intelligently. In this stage, it is important to diminish the amount of scaffolding and direction, provide more interesting and complex problems, and use performance based tasks to permit students to explore a variety of solutions.

To develop competence in consultation, students require the opportunity to apply the skills they have learned in real situations under supervision that gradually enables the student to become more independent. The setting for the application of skills is the schools. Fieldwork assignments are arranged in settings with field supervisors who are experienced in consultation service delivery and who are working in schools where consultation is a major part of their role. The field supervisor models consultation practices, and also assists the student consultant in finding appropriate consultees and coping with school placement issues. However, it should be noted that the field supervisor does not provide the bulk of the individual supervision on consultation sessions; the major supervision responsibility is at the university level.

By the end of the first semester, students have applied their skills in several sessions with an actual consultee under close supervision from a university-based supervisor. Each consultation session is taped, with the informed consent of the teacher consultee, and the student is required to prepare a log of the session for the course instructor and supervisor, reflecting on the progress of the consultation and their own performance. In the second course, students are assigned at least two consultation cases with one or more teachers.

Since the second course also covers organizational consultation concepts, a systems level consultation project, again with university-based supervision, is developed. Student consultants have engaged in projects such as developing cross-age peer tutoring systems, participating in school discipline committee activities, enhancing team functioning, or administrative consultation with building principals about concerns. Moreover, students are introduced to effective teaming practices and parent consultation at the awareness and conceptual understanding level.

Supervision

Supervision is critical for building skill competence, yet little has been written about supervision of consultation skills. Stoltenberg (1993) noted that reaching potential as a consultant requires "supervised experience across a number of environments over an extended period of time" (p. 139), but that "the increase in course work and training in consultation has not been accompanied by a systematic approach to training or extended across the developmental stages of supervisee competence" (p. 132).

Bernard and Goodyear (1998) presented four types of supervision interventions, including self-report, process notes, audiotape and videotape, indicating the strengths and weaknesses of each. They suggest that both self-report and process notes do not allow the supervisor to independently judge what occurred during the sessions, and are not sufficient at the early stage of skill development. They view these modes of supervision as limited by the conceptual and observational abilities of the supervisee. Neither self-report nor process notes allow the supervisor to address communication skills.

According to Bernard and Goodyear (1998), the strength of audiotaping is that the supervisor and supervisee can accurately hear what occurred during the session, allowing them to focus on process, content and communication skills. The effect of audiotaping on supervision of consultation was captured in an exchange between a supervisor and supervisee, discussing a problematic situation in a consultation case:

Supervisee: That's what I was trying to say—just to paraphrase what she had said. But I said, it doesn't look like he was using the knowledge that he has. Which isn't even related.

Supervisor: To what she meant, uh-huh.

Supervisee: And it's not even—it wasn't even close to what she said. But I didn't realize that at all until we played that {section of the tape}...I still would have trouble saying it, but—

Supervisor: I definitely understand what you mean and that's the reason that ...people transcribe and then write next to—you know, what they were actually thinking or what they thought they were saying or what they wanted to be saying, because so often the two don't match.

Supervisee: Yeah. I completely—and I wouldn't have picked it up unless you actually said something about that. I think I do that a lot though. I'm not as clear as I think I am.....

Supervisor: I think, I think it's difficult to be clear in the moment and I think it's easy to criticize yourself....it's cause you're trying to formulate something in your head as you're speaking and ah, it's not easy to do. It's really not and that's why this practice is good.

Although the benefits of using tapes in consultation supervision are enormous, a survey of consultation training in school psychology programs (Anton & Rosenfield, 2000), to which faculty members teaching consultation in nearly half of the school psychology training programs in the United States responded, revealed relatively little regular taping of consultation sessions for supervision. Results indicated that 17% of the respondents required taping of consultation sessions and only 9% of those reviewed their tapes with a supervisor on a regular basis.

Given the consultee-centered nature of IC, the language systems focus, and the need to develop both content and process expertise, audiotaping for supervision has been integrated into the training of instructional consultants, beginning with the first assigned case. Cramer, Rosenfield, Mewborn, Anton, and Schulmeyer (2001), as part of a workshop on consultation supervision, presented case studies of how audiotaping provided unique opportunities for student consultants to explore consultation skill development in process, content and communication domains. In one case, the student consultee believed she was being "too pushy" during a session. Listening to the tape enabled her to talk more objectively about her interactions. Role-playing in supervision, based on actual teacher comments, enabled another supervisee to learn how to present her own ideas on topics where basic assumptions between consultant and consultee differed. Subtle changes in the teacher's conception of the case could be traced through the teacher's language on the tape, providing support to the student consultant that she was indeed making progress. In several instances, the tape enabled a supervisor to help the supervisee with content information that the supervisee was unaware was important.

Finally, a supervisor can assist supervisees with more sophisticated use of communication skills. For example, student consultants are often confused about how to use communication skills such as clarification. Or, student consultants may report that they have made a point that the teacher is resistant to hearing. However, in listening to the tape, it becomes clear that the comments were too tangential for the teacher to understand. In one case, it was possible for the supervisee to develop strategies to make her actual words more congruent with her intentions, and to do so in ways that were possible for the teacher to hear (Cramer et al., 2001). Thus, in terms of content knowledge, interpersonal skills, and communication skills, supervision utilized the audiotape for supervisee growth.

Although in this author's experience these results are not unusual, research on the value of audiotaping on consultant skill development should be pursued. This is essential since the use of individual supervision of consultation, using audiotapes, is highly resource intensive for training programs. Consultation case supervision is delivered at the university by the course instructor, experienced consultant practitioners, or advanced graduate students who are supervised by the course instructor. A graduate assistant estimated that she spent 6–7 hours per week supervising four students. This included listening to tapes, meeting with students in pairs, and preparing for and receiving her own supervision.

At the conclusion of the two-course sequence in consultation, the student has had the opportunity to acquire basic knowledge on skills needed and to receive supervised experience with two to three teacher consultees in school sites in which consultation is routinely practiced. School psychology students take the two-course sequence during their second year, while graduate students from other disciplines generally take the first course as an elective in their program. The university supervisor through listening to student tapes, reading logs and final report summaries, and discussion with on-site supervisors evaluates competence in the application of consultation skills.

Proficiency—Expertise

Expertise or proficiency is the highest stage of domain knowledge. Professionals at this stage are formulating knowledge in the area, and exploring problems that stimulate their minds and engage their interest (Alexander, 1997). Learners should be encouraged to formulate alternative perspectives or to frame novel problems that can guide personal exploration. Additional practice with appropriate supervision, supervision of less experienced consultants, and research projects provide opportunities to move toward expertise in this domain.

At the advanced skill acquisition level, doctoral students who wish to become more expert in IC and systems consultation do a third year fieldwork experience, 1 day per week, in a school where consultation is routinely practiced. Fieldwork students typically continue to tape their sessions. They receive supervision from a university-based faculty member and an on-site supervisor. Both doctoral and nondoctoral students also have the opportunity to do their internship in school systems where professionals routinely practice consultation. The school-based internship supervisor provides supervision. Internship experiences are typically not taped and interns do not receive the intense supervision done at the university (Cramer et al., 2001). Programs that anticipate that students will receive more training on consultation during their internships need to recognize the limited nature of consultation supervision in the field. Commonly, interns may have the opportunity to consult, but do not receive the degree of feedback that novice consultants need to achieve competence, much less expertise, in this domain.

Another way to enhance skill acquisition is through supervision of beginning consultants. Anton and Rosenfield's (2000) study of consultation training indicated that nearly 20% of those supervising students in consultation courses received no training in supervision, and few respondents had course work in supervision. To provide a cadre of consultation supervisors, advanced graduate students are invited to supervise beginning consultation students under close supervision from university faculty. Advanced students report that supervising novice consultants allows them to solidify their skills.

For those who select to move into more advanced consultation skill development, there are opportunities to conduct research on consultation. Engagement in research allows consultants to develop new knowledge and stimulate personal exploration, described by Alexander (1997) as critical to this stage. It also provides a cadre of experts to advance the consultation domain.

IMPLICATIONS FOR CONSULTATION PRACTICE

There is considerable effort to encourage collaboration and problem solving in schools, partly in response to IDEA requirements to evaluate how well students have been instructed and partly because of the recognition of the efficacy of improved support services prior to special education referral. However in asking practitioners to adopt any set of professional practices, it is essential that they be, and believe themselves to be, competent in the skills required (Rosenfield, 2000a). We have not sufficiently attended to the process of how practitioners move from novice to competent to expert in consultation, and consultation training itself has received scant attention in our training programs. Crego (1985) noted the haphazard nature of consultation training, "uneven across specialty fields within psychology, and generally unguided by education and training standards" (p. 474).

Hellkamp, Zins, Ferguson and Hodge (1998), having surveyed applied psychology programs, agreed on the limited number of "courses, practicum experiences or workshops on consulting, regardless of specialty area" (p. 235). According to Anton and Rosenfield (2000), while the majority of school psychology programs offer one course in consultation, less than 10% of the nondoctoral programs and only 25% of doctoral programs offer two courses. Although this is clearly a positive change from Stewart's 1985 data, which indicated that only 66% of doctoral students and 39% of nondoctoral students received any consultation training at all, students have usually developed awareness and conceptual understanding, but only limited skills after one course. In confirmation, Guest (2000) found that nearly 30% of novice school psychologists feel they have received "insufficient training and/or expertise in a range of skills" (p. 243) related to consultation. Crego (1985) noted the "dramatic increase in formal consultation course work... and experiential training in some doctoral training programs" (p. 474), but again commented on the lack of training that is "systemic or extended over developmental stages of trainee competence" (p. 474).

In addition, there is little in our literature that addresses how to ensure that fledgling practitioners enter into practice communities where consultation services are routinely and competently practiced. In fact, one of my goals in working with nearby school systems has been to establish school sites that would allow students in consultation courses to see consultation and data based problem solving as the model routinely used by practitioners. It is important to address how to increase the level and quality of consultation training in our programs, and relatedly, how to increase the amount of consultation done in practice (Rosenfield, 2000a).

Although the amount and intensity of training presented here may seem high, it is more comparable to that received by school psychology students in psychoeducational assessment. If school psychologists and other school professionals are to be as comfortable in the complex skills of consultation as in other skills, there needs to be more attention to training.

How much training at the graduate level, however, is an empirical question. The IC-Team Lab at the University of Maryland is evaluating models of training at the inservice level for school-based professionals (see Gravois et al., this issue), as well as distance learning technology involving taping and case supervision. Recognizing the need for advanced training, Crego (1985) suggested exploring organized post-doctoral training in consultation.

In Sum

According to a recent survey of training programs (Anton & Rosenfield, 2000), IC has emerged, after behavioral and mental health consultation, as the third most common model of consultation taught in school psychology training programs. The major dimensions of IC have been described here and a sequence for developing consultants presented. Education begins with awareness and conceptual understanding, and skill acquisition during the acclimation stage. It progresses to application of skills in practice setting under close supervision, which builds toward competency. Advanced skills and proficiency emerge during extended opportunities for practice, supervision activities and research among those who become interested in developing expertise in this domain. Most professional programs provide only limited opportunities for the development of competency and expertise. A stronger emphasis on quality training in consultation is required for this domain of practice to achieve its full potential.

REFERENCES

Alexander, P. A. (1997). Mapping the multidimensional nature of domain learning: The interplay of cognitive, motivational and strategic forces. *Advances in Motivation and Achievement, 10,* 213–250.
Anton, J. M., & Rosenfield, S. (2000, March). *A survey of preservice consultation training and supervision.* Poster session presented at the National Association of School Psychologists, New Orleans, LA.

Bernard, J. M., & Goodyear, R. K. (1998). *Fundamentals of clinical supervision*. Needham Heights, MA: Allyn & Bacon.

Bloom, B. S. (1976). *Human characteristics and school learning*. New York: McGraw Hill.

Caplan, G. (1970). *The theory and practice of mental health consultation*. New York: Basic Books.

Cramer, K., Rosenfield, S., Mewborn, K., Anton, J., & Schulmeyer, C. (2001, April). *The process of supervision in consultation for everyone involved*. Mini-skills workshop presented at the National Association of School Psychologists, Washington, DC.

Cramer, K., & Rosenfield, S. (1999). Module #6: Understanding how to use curriculum-based assessment. (Web-based self-study module). National Association of School Psychologists: http://w.w.w.naspweb.org/certification/ss_module6.html.

Crego, C. A. (1985). Ethics: The need for improved consultation training. *The Counseling Psychologist, 13*, 473–476.

Gravois, T. A., & Gickling, E. E. (2002). Best practices in Curriculum-Based Assessment. In A. Thomas & J. Grimes (Eds.), *Best practices in school psychology-IV* (pp. 885–898). Washington, DC: National Association of School Psychologists.

Gravois, T. A., Rosenfield, S., & Vail, P. L. (1999). Achieving effective and inclusive school settings: A guide for professional development. *Special Services in the Schools, 15*, 145–170.

Guest, K. E. (2000). Career development of school psychologists. *Journal of School Psychology, 38*, 237–257.

Hellkamp, D. T., Zins, J. E., Ferguson, K., & Hodge, M. (1998). Training practices in consultation: A national survey of clinical, counseling, industrial/organizational, and school psychology faculty. *Consulting Psychology Journal: Practice and Research, 50*, 228–236.

Higgins, E. T. (1999). "Saying is believing" effects: When sharing reality about something biases knowledge and evaluations. In L. L. Thompson, J. M. Levine, & D. M. Messick (Eds.), *Shared cognition in organizations* (pp. 33–48). Mahwah, NJ: Lawrence Erlbaum Associates, Inc.

Jones, G. (1999). *Validation of a simulation to evaluate instructional consultation problem identification skill competence*. Dissertation Abstracts International, 51(00A)3018. (University Microfilms No. AAG9034633).

Joyce, B., & Showers, B. (1980). Improving inservice training: The messages of research. *Educational Leadership, 37*, 379–385.

Rosenfield, S. (1987). *Instructional consultation*. Mahwah, NJ: Lawrence Erlbaum Associates, Inc.

Rosenfield, S. (1995). The practice of instructional consultation. *Journal of Educational and Psychological Consultation, 6*, 317–327.

Rosenfield, S. (1999, June). *Developing skills in the language systems approach to consultee-centered consultation*. Paper presented at the Second International Seminar on Consultee-Centered Consultation, Stockholm, Sweden.

Rosenfield, S. (2000a). Commentary on Sheridan and Gutkin: Unfinished Business. *School Psychology Review, 29*, 505–506.

Rosenfield, S. (2000b). Crafting usable knowledge. *American Psychologist, 55*, 1347–1355.

Rosenfield, S. (2002). Best practices in instructional Consultation. In A. Thomas & J. Grimes (Eds.), *Best practices in school psychology* (Vol. 4, pp. 609–623). Washington, DC: National Association of School Psychologists.

Rosenfield, S., & Gravois, T. A. (1996). *Instructional consultation teams: Collaborating for change*. New York: Guilford.

Stewart (1985, August). *Academic consultation: Differences in doctoral and non-doctoral training and practice.* Paper presented at the annual meeting of the American Psychological Association, Los Angeles, CA.

Stoltenberg, C. D. (1993). Supervising consultants in training: An application of a model of supervision. *Journal of Counseling and Development, 72,* 131–139.

Tarakan, L. M. (1996). *The development of self-assessment problem identification rating scales for instructional consultation training.* Unpublished master's thesis, University of Maryland, College Park.

White, L., Summerlin, M. L., Loos, V., & Epstein, E. (1992). School and family consultation: A language-systems approach. In M. Fine & C. Carlson (Eds.), *Handbook of family-school interventions: A systems perspective* (pp. 347–362). Boston: Allyn & Bacon.

Ysseldyke, J., & Christenson, S. (2002). *Functional assessment of academic behavior.* Longmont, CO: Sopris West.

Sylvia Rosenfield is professor of school psychology at the University of Maryland, College Park. Her research interests include instructional consultation/instructional consultation teams, educating consultants, and implementation of change in the schools.

JOURNAL OF EDUCATIONAL AND PSYCHOLOGICAL CONSULTATION, 13(1&2), 113–132
Copyright © 2002, Lawrence Erlbaum Associates, Inc.

Educating Practitioners as Consultants: Development and Implementation of the Instructional Consultation Team Consortium

Todd A. Gravois
University of Maryland

Steve Knotek and Leslie M. Babinski
Bucknell University

The continuing education of current practitioners as consultants is an area requiring both practical consideration and further research. The Instructional Consultation Team (IC-Team) Consortium represents a comprehensive, statewide effort to systematically train a diverse group of educational practitioners as instructional consultants within the context of a team service delivery model. This article describes the IC-Team Consortium and summarizes the empirically based professional development process used to support practitioners' consultation skill development and application. The article summarizes the multi-tiered system of professional development that includes an intense introductory training of consultation skills followed by a structured process of coaching during application. In addition, the article describes the use of the IC-Team as an arena for team members' continued development of consultation skills.

The focus of inservice education of practitioners in the area of consultation has received minimal attention (Reschly, 1993). Even though educating individuals as consultants within the preservice arena is a complex process

Correspondence should be addressed to Todd A. Gravois, Department of Counseling and Personnel Services, 3214 Benjamin Building, University of Maryland, College Park, MD 20742.

deserving attention (J. Meyers, this issue), the difficulty of this process is compounded when considering the education of current practitioners. Whereas preservice students are often motivated by grades or the attainment of a degree, practitioners vary in their motivation for continued learning and often are faced with the real demands of carrying out current job responsibilities while attempting to learn new skills. Furthermore, current practitioners who are motivated to learn, develop and apply consultation skills are often faced with an organizational environment that itself is not supportive of change (Reschly, 1993).

The development of effective consultation skills for educational practitioners represents a critical need and is the focus of this article. First we describe an empirically based framework of professional development essential in developing consultation skills, whether it be for preservice students or practitioners. Next, the article details the development and implementation of a statewide effort to systematically "re-tool" practitioners' service delivery through the introduction of a particular model of consultation-based teaming, Instructional Consultation Teams (IC-Teams; Rosenfield & Gravois, 1996). Finally, we describe the training model for IC-Teams as one example of a comprehensive continuing education program designed to develop consultation skills for a variety of educational practitioners (i.e., psychologists, counselors, classroom teachers, special educators, etc.).

FRAMEWORK FOR CONTINUING
EDUCATION OF CONSULTANTS

In the 1970s, educational researchers demonstrated that fewer than 10% of participants involved in workshop or inservice programs implemented what they learned (Showers & Joyce, 1996). Such lack of transfer represents a critical challenge for those attempting to assist practitioners in developing and applying skills as consultants. However, recent attention to the practices and procedures utilized in training and inservice have significantly increased the likelihood of acquisition of new skills and knowledge, and the ultimate transfer of skills into practice. In their classic review of the literature, Joyce and Showers (1980) suggested four methods of training that should be considered and integrated into a well designed professional development program. Each method of training provides a different level of impact on professionals' skill, knowledge and practice. Table 1 provides a summary of various training methods and the associated level of impact on participants' development of knowledge and skills.

TABLE 1
Training Methods and Impact Upon Participants

Training Method	Level of Impact	Evidence of Impact
Didactic presentation of theory and concepts	Awareness	Participant can articulate general concepts and identify problem
Modeling and demonstration (i.e., live, video, etc.)	Conceptual understanding	Participant can articulate concepts clearly and describe appropriate actions required
Practice in simulated situations with Feedback (i.e., role play, written exercises, etc.)	Skill acquisition	Participant can begin to use skills in structured or simulated situations
Coaching and supervision during application	Application of skills	Participants can use skills flexibly in actual situation

Of particular challenge in continuing education programs is the ability to go beyond the first three levels of impact (i.e., awareness, understanding, and development of skills in isolation) and achieve the ultimate goal of assisting practitioners apply newly learned skills in daily work activities (see also Rosenfield, this issue). Showers, Joyce, and Bennett (1987) demonstrated that the on-going use of coaching produces significant transfer of newly acquired skills and knowledge into actual practice. Indeed, the lack of on-going support during application may actually have a negative impact on practitioners' motivation to remain engaged in future training and professional development (Hawley & Valli, 1999).

THE CHALLENGE OF PROVIDING CONTINUING EDUCATION TO PRACTITIONERS

The challenge of creating either a coaching or supervision component is especially elusive in the area of developing consultation skills (see Rosenfield, this issue). An example of this challenge is seen in school psychology training. Although "School Psychology: A Blueprint for Training and Practice II" (Ysseldyke et al., 1997) lists consultation as one of the most critical skills for school psychologists to develop, relatively few university programs (10% nondoctoral and 25% doctoral) offer more than one semester of school consultation coursework (Anton & Rosenfield, 2000). One semester of coursework may acclimate students to consultation, but the limited time frame significantly reduces the opportunity for a full compliment of training methods, including supervised practice of application in real cases (Rosenfield, this issue). As Rosenfield suggests, the practice of consultation, being a complex integration of skills, certainly requires a component that allows multiple applications with feedback and guidance to achieve a level of competence that would be considered beyond the novice level. If sufficient opportunity for feedback during application is difficult to accomplish within preservice training programs, it is hard to imagine such comprehensive training in consultation occurring at the inservice or practitioner level that can achieve much more than acclimation.

Although support during the application of newly learned consultation skills remains important, the literature related to inservice programs for educating consultants (e.g., Idol & West, 1987; McDougall, Reschly, & Corkery, 1988; Reschly, 1993), often provides only brief descriptions of how and when application is either supervised or coached. However there are practices, such as on-line supervision and coaching (e.g., Kruger, Cohen, Marca & Matthews, 1996) that offer promise in the effective development of consultation skills for practitioners. The critical need for trainers of practitioners then, is to strategically combine and match training methods, including some form of feedback during application, to the participants' entry skill and knowledge to produce the greatest impact and change in practice (Joyce & Showers, 1980, Showers & Joyce, 1996). The creation of just such a comprehensive staff development program in consultation has been and continues to be the goal of the IC-Team training model.

INSTRUCTIONAL CONSULTATION TEAMS

Although it is not possible to fully describe the IC-Team model within the scope of this article, there are several characteristics of the model relevant to our discussion of developing consultation skills in current practitioners (see Rosenfield & Gravois, 1996, for a full description of the IC-Team model). First, IC-Teams represent a system of early intervention with a primary focus on resolving student learning and behavioral concerns within the general education classroom by offering support to teachers. The team utilizes a consultation-based service delivery system requiring each team member to develop and apply consultation skills. Each team member serves as a case manager (consultant) to an individual teacher who has requested assistance (see Figure 1). This service delivery structure shifts the focus away from group or team problem solving toward the dyadic relationship between one team member and the teacher (i.e., a consultant–consultee relationship).

Second, IC-Teams seek to develop a well-functioning multidisciplinary team by focusing on the development of individual team members' skills. The goal is to go beyond the traditional emphasis on group problem-solving skills as seen with many team models (Rosenfield & Gravois, 1999). Instead, the team becomes a context for the development of individual team members' skills as instructional consultants. Weekly team meetings serve both as a problem-solving arena for case discussion to support success for teachers and students, and also ensure that each team member develops necessary skills for effective consultation. This approach to team development seeks to minimize practitioners' development of consultation skills in isolation from

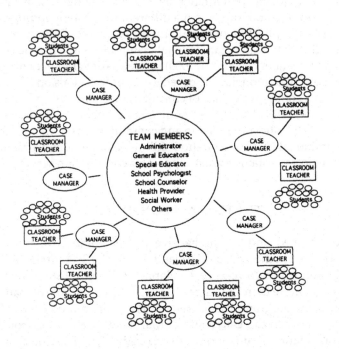

FIGURE 1   Instructional consultation team service delivery configuration.

other professionals' functioning. Since all team members are engaged in developing a common concept of consultation, a common barrier of facilitating effective collaboration and problem solving among a diverse group of professionals is also addressed (McMahon, Ward, Pruett, Davidson, & Griffith, 2000; Rosenfield & Gravois, 1999).

Third, the IC-Team serves to directly confront the existing culture of the school organization and support the application of consultation services by practitioners. Even though consultation remains an emphasized form of service delivery, the reality remains that such services are still considered secondary to traditional practices (e.g., refer-test-place) and are difficult to establish within schools (Costenbader, Swartz, & Petrix, 1992; Reschly, 2000; Reschly & Wilson, 1995). For example, in Reschly's (1993) summary of RE-AIM, a program to develop consultation skills of practicing psychologists and special educators, the application of consultation skills by participants was less than 10% in some districts to over 75% in others. The variance of application was thought to be related to the support provided to the practitioner by the employing school system or agency to develop and implement a different role. These findings suggest that increased application of consultation as a service delivery model will require both a change in organizational assumptions and policies (see, e.g., Zins, Elias, Greenberg, & Pruett, 2000), as well as development of skills and knowledge of practitioners. The diversity of professionals on IC-Teams, all engaged in a common practice of consultation, creates what Fullan (2001) referred to as "critical mass" —a sufficient number and representation of the school staff "who are skilled in and committed to the change" (p. 89). It is this commonality of consultation skill development and practices that attempts to foster organizational support for consultation service delivery.

THE IC-TEAM CONSORTIUM

The most refined and comprehensive implementation of the IC-Team model occurred in the state of Maryland during the 2000–2001 school year, following more than 15 years of development. Twenty-three school teams, comprised of more than 250 school-based processionals participated in the first year of the program. The IC-Team Consortium represents a collaborative effort between the University of Maryland's Laboratory for Instructional Consultation Teams and seven school districts. The Consortium was formed after district personnel requested assistance in coordinating and providing continuing education, technical support, and program development to foster consultation-based services for teachers and students. Specifically, several administrators from multiple districts had approached the University to seek assistance with somewhat varied, but related concerns. For example, one director of special education had become aware of the IC-Team program in an adjacent district and of the resulting impact on reduction of special education evaluations and placements. His desire was to create a more effective program of early intervention to address his own district's increasing evaluation and placement rates. An assistant superintendent of instruction from another district contacted the university to address her district's recent data related to the overidentification of minority students in special education. In yet another district, the director of pupil services was interested in developing school-based teams that engaged classroom teachers in the support process rather than simply being a vehicle for documenting paperwork and recommending strategies prior to decision making for special education.

In addition, each district had funding sources available that targeted particular populations of students or professional development of teachers, but few of the individual funding sources were sufficient in themselves to formulate a comprehensive approach to servicing students and teachers. For example, one district had several sources of funding targeting specific school and student needs. There were funds for students of poverty, funds for addressing the overidentification of minority students in special education, funds for professional development and funds for students considered at-risk for school failure. What was missing was a conceptual framework for service delivery that met the specific needs of the targeted student populations and promoted professional development to teachers and staff beyond the individual funding source requirements.

Funding for the IC-Team Consortium was derived from the various training and technical support grants mentioned previously (e.g., to fund workshop and substitute stipends for team members participation in training) and also from each local district's operating budgets (e.g., to provide increased psychologists' time to serve as team facilitators). Finally, coordination funding was derived from the federal Goals 2000 Act (1994) grant program with a supplement provided by the state's Office of Special Education services. This 3-year grant was designed to combine available funding and provide additional funds to coordinate training, technical support and program evaluation across all participating districts.

The IC-Team Consortium was developed to serve two purposes. First, the collaborative initiative between university and school professionals is designed to assist school districts in developing and implementing effective consultation-based services to serve students and teachers within selected schools. Once personnel are trained and the teams implemented, these schools serve as demonstration and training sites within the local education agency (LEA) to support future expansion to additional schools and potential placement sites for preservice consultation students. The second purpose of the IC-Team Consortium is to develop systematically the technical expertise and capacity of district personnel so over time each LEA may effectively implement and evaluate consultation-based services.

A major component of the IC-Team Consortium is the use of an on-site team facilitator to support the development of individual team members' skills in consultation. Although school psychologists have been the primary professional to assume the team facilitator role, other professionals, such as counselors, special educators and social workers have also served as team facilitators. Regardless of the professional assuming the role, the IC-Team Facilitator receives staff development in advance of the other team members and participates in the full compliment of training described in Table 1 to develop the necessary skills as an instructional consultant. In addition, the facilitator receives extensive professional development in critical change facilitation skills (Rosenfield & Gravois, 1996; Saxl, Lieberman, & Miles 1987; Vail, Gravois & Rosenfield, 2001) to support the development of consultation skills of all team members.

University-based trainers and consultants provide training and technical support to both IC-Team Facilitators and, in the initial phase, to the IC-Teams themselves. As professional development progresses, university support is targeted more toward the development of IC-Team Facilitator skills with less direct interaction with the school-based IC-Teams themselves. The ultimate goal is for teams to become self-directed and proficient in designing continued professional development of consultation skills for existing and new members. In some larger districts, an IC-Team District Facilitator might be employed to coordinate implementation across a large number of schools within that particular LEA.

PROFESSIONAL DEVELOPMENT IN INSTRUCTIONAL CONSULTATION

The development of consultation skills for practitioners within the IC-Team Consortium uses empirically based principles of professional development (Joyce & Showers,1980; Showers & Joyce, 1996) and parallels the training often described for preservice consultation students (e.g., Gallesich, 1983; Idol, 1993; Meyers, this issue; Rosenfield, this issue). However, as would be expected, the delivery of training and logistical support for application represents a unique challenge when working in the applied setting. Differences in practitioner motivation, prior experience, employment demands, and external supports for changing service delivery only add to the complexity already documented in the inservice training of consultants.

The IC-Team Consortium uses a multi-tiered system of professional development to ensure the achievement of the ultimate goal—that of impacting participants' development and application of consultation skills (Gallesich, 1983). An introductory institute consisting of 20–25 hours of didactic and simulated activities is used to provide awareness, understanding and beginning skill development for all participants. A "coaching during application phase" follows this institute. The premise of the IC-Team Consortium's professional development sequence is to address the known challenges in consultation training in the applied setting, and offer on-going, comprehensive support to address those challenges that will likely arise.

IC-Team Institute

All IC-Team Facilitators and IC-Team members participate in the same introductory week long institute held primarily in the summer (fall and winter institutes are held periodically to accommodate needs of district personnel). However, IC-Team Facilitators' professional development sequence begins 3 months to 1 year in advance of the remaining team members and includes an intense skill application and coaching component. When team training does occur, all members (as displayed in Figure 1) are expected to attend as a unified team.

The goal of the institute is to create a shared awareness and understanding of the IC-Team model, its critical assumptions, processes and structures. Critical instructional consultation (Rosenfield, 1987, 2002) competencies are introduced and developed during this training including collaborative communication skills (Gutkin & Curtis, 1982), ecobehavioral stage-based problem solving (Gutkin & Curtis, 1999), curriculum based assessment (Gravois & Gickling, 2002), functional behavioral assessment and the collection, analysis and charting of academic and behavioral data. Figure 2 provides an agenda of the 4-day institute detailing the content and professional development techniques (in bold print). Throughout, professional development includes a focus on empirically based learning and behavioral principles that underlie effective instruction and classroom management

DAY 1	DAY 2	DAY 3	DAY 4
Welcome & Overview of Training	Collaborative Communication Skills (continued) *(Didactic Presentation, Written Activity, Videotaped Model & Practice with Structured Feedback)*	CBA (continued)	Stage 3: Intervention Design and Strategy Development *(Didactic Presentation & Experiential Activity)*
Goals and Objectives of Instructional Consultation Teams		Integration of Communication Skills, CBA and Problem-Solving Stages	Stages 4 & 5: Intervention Implementation and Evaluation and Case Closure *(Didactic Presentation)*
Awareness of Change *(Experiential Activity with Reflective Discussion)*	Overview of Problem Solving Stages *(Didactic Presentation)*	Stage 1: Contracting *(Demonstration and Practice with Structured Feedback)*	Integration of Skills: Case Study *(Written and Experiential Activities with Reflective Discussion)*
Key IC Assumptions *(Experiential Activity with Reflective Discussion and Didactic Presentation)*	Curriculum Based Assessment *(Experiential Activity with Reflective Discussion , Didactic Presentation Videotaped Model & Written Practice with Structured Feedback)*	Stage 2: Problem Identification and Analysis *(Videotaped Model, Written Activity and Practice with Structured Feedback)*	Behavioral Assessment Linked to Problem Solving Stages *(Didactic Presentation)*
Collaborative Communication Skills *(Experiential Activity with Reflective Discussion)*		Charting & Graphing Data *(Written Model, Didactic Presentation & Practice with Feedback)*	Planning for On-Line Follow-up or IC-Team Functioning *(Didactic, Videotaped Model, Written Activity)*

FIGURE 2   IC-Team Consortium Institute agenda.

(Gravois & Gickling, 2002; Gravois, Rosenfield, & Vail, 1999; Rosenfield, 1987).

An important part of the institute is to facilitate exploration of the underlying assumptions associated with instructional consultation and compare and contrast these with other approaches for addressing student learning difficulties. For example, participants are challenged to differentiate the common practice of identifying learning problems as internally-based student deficits (i.e., traditional special education eligibility) with the ecological view posed by the instructional consultation model that the match between instruction, student entry skills and curricula demands should be the focus of problem solving.

Multiple components are used to support the attendees' acquisition of consultation skills and is reflective of the competency based training used by Kratochwill and his colleagues to prepare school psychologists in behavioral consultation (Kratochwill, Sheridan, Rotto, & Salmon, 1992). During the week long institute, didactic presentation is utilized to introduce the theory and empirical bases underlying instructional consultation and assist participants in developing an awareness and initial understanding of the key components and skills involved in this particular model of consultation. A comprehensive training manual (Gravois, Rosenfield & Gickling, 1998) as well as in-depth reference material (e.g., Rosenfield, 1987; Rosenfield & Gravois, 1996) provide uniformity and integrity of training. Written exercises and demonstrations (i.e., videotaped consultation sessions) assist in deepening participants' understanding of the consultation process. Role-play activities with accompanying feedback and ample opportunities for reflective discussion target the development and application of skills within simulated situations.

The fundamental task of consultation training programs is to provide for the initial and ongoing means for novices to acquire and master core competencies (Kratochwill, Sheridan, Rotto, & Salmon, 1991) and skills (Zins, Curtis, Graden, & Ponti, 1989). The IC-Team institute seeks to meet this challenge by creating a respectful atmosphere that allows experienced practitioners to examine existing beliefs, knowledge and skills, while learning the skills and knowledge associated with becoming an instructional consultant within a larger team model. One example of a difficulty in meeting this challenge is in the need to differentiate the IC-Team case consultant structure from the traditional group problem-solving formats that operate in most schools. The reality is, with the exception of participants who are classroom teachers, most of the other professionals (i.e., psychologists, special educators, principals, etc.) attending the institute have long and varied histories of being involved in school-based teams. Unfortunately, much of participants' experiences have occurred with little or no professional development in effective teaming practices or they have participated on teams whose primary purpose focused on deciding whether children are suspected of having disabilities rather than problem-solve student and teacher concerns. Such experiences have resulted in participants having little enthusiasm for consultation-based services or the hope of achieving true problem solving within schools.

A second, and possibly more important challenge is the need to address the variation of participants' preservice training in and application of consultation. There is a need to acknowledge entry consultation skills, while at the same time assist participants in critically assessing and evaluating their skill development needs. Although some team members have been exposed to consultation as part of preservice preparation (i.e., psychologists, special educators, counselors, etc.) others (i.e., classroom teachers) have limited or no exposure. This variation in entry skills is further confounded when considering that those participants who have received as part of preservice exposure to consultation often vary in the models of consultation introduced, and in their actual skill application and supervision within preservice training (see Rosenfield, this issue). The discrepancy between participants' conceptual knowledge and actual skill development is often revealed during participation in experiential activities within the training. To this end, small group interactions within the institute allow for continuous and peer supported reflection so practitioners can comfortably acknowledge skill development needs.

Coaching During Skill Application

The ability to provide feedback and promote professional reflection during the application of newly learned skills represents one of the greatest logistical and resource challenges in the continuing education of consultants. Coaching during application is widely cited in the professional development of teaching skills (e.g., Caccia, 1996; Garmston, 1987; Joyce & Showers, 1996) and offers a vehicle to provide structured feedback during the development of consultation skills by practitioners. The IC-Team Consortium utilizes two coaching components as part of the development of individual consultation skills. These two components include an on-line coaching process and a face-to-face on-site coaching process.

On-line coaching. The on-line coaching component is designed for those participants receiving advanced training in instructional consultation and who ultimately serve as the IC-Team facilitator. This component utilizes a technical coaching model (Garmston, 1987) with structured observation and feedback and is intended to assist the transfer of skills learned in the institute into practice. Because the goal of technical coaching is to increase the use of a particular strategy or skill, the data collection format and subsequent feedback is often specific to evaluating the acquisition and application of the particular consultation skill or strategy. The coach generally is observing for the presence or absence, and quality of the newly acquired skill.

On completing the summer institute, participants return to their home school and apply their skills within an actual consultation case with a classroom teacher. All case sessions are audiotaped and reviewed by a coach trained and experienced in instructional consultation. The coach reviews the taped session and accompanying documentation of the case and provides structured feedback via e-mail (e.g., Kruger & Struzziero, 1997) on a weekly basis.

Even though on-line feedback for training is only beginning to be explored within the literature (Myric & Sabell, 1995; Spitzer & Wedding,

1995), there are positive features that address the challenges of providing feedback about practitioners' application of consultation skills. For example, since e-mail is asynchronous (i.e., coach and participant are not on-line at the same time), it provides greater flexibility for coach and participant in terms of sending and receiving feedback. Since a majority of the IC-Team Consortium participants are full-time practitioners and have professional and personal demands on their time, e-mail represents a format that can be easily accessed at their convenience from home rather than a scheduled meeting at some distant location. In addition to the flexibility noted in using e-mail, IC-Team participants indicate that the text-based communication offered greater opportunities to reflect on the feedback provided since allowed them to review and re-read the e-mails prior to their next session. Such comments are consistent with the findings of research investigating graduate students engaged in distance learning coursework (Maxwell & McCain, 1995).

Although a majority of e-mail coaching used in the IC-Team Consortium is asynchronous, coaches and participants have arranged synchronized communication when necessary. The consortium is currently experimenting with secured synchronized (i.e., chat room discussions) formats that allow real-time discussion among coaches and participants as well as discussion boards in which all coaches and participants can post questions for general support. It is our hope that the expansion of such options for coaches and participants will increase the opportunity for providing feedback during application of consultation skills.

The logistical benefits of using e-mail as part of the coaching process have been seen throughout the IC-Team consortium. However, the impact of using such technology on consultant skill acquisition and application remains limited and requires further research. The advantages in using on-line coaching in the IC-Team Consortium have been the ability to overcome the logistical difficulty of providing coaching to practitioners in remote or distant locales and the resulting efficiency in use of training resources. The major dilemma has been the time-lag resulting from mailing tapes from practitioner to coach. With the continued advance of technology, there is hope for real-time recording of consultation in one locale to be transmitted electronically to the coach and then subsequently providing a wide-range of feedback options to support the coaching experience.

On-site coaching.   The second coaching component of the IC-Team Consortium builds on the first. By providing advanced training and coaching to the IC-Team Facilitator, along with additional skill in change facilitation and coaching, the IC-Team Facilitator assumes the role of on-site coach for other team members as they apply newly learned consultation skills. Coaching is provided to individual team members as they begin application of the problem-solving model within actual consultation cases.

The model of coaching employed on-site between the facilitator and team members is best described as collegial or peer coaching (Garmston, 1987). Unlike technical coaching, collegial coaching occurs between peers (i.e., IC-Team Facilitator and IC-Team member) who voluntarily engage in a three phase coaching process to improve and develop consultation skills. The coaching process typically consists of three steps, a preconference phase, a data collection phase and a coaching conference (Rosenfield & Gravois, 1996).

In the preconference, the IC-Team Facilitator and team member identify a particular area of consultation skill to focus on. Next, there is agreement as to the specific types of data that are needed to provide information on the use or application of the identified consultation skill. Data collection for coaching purposes varies greatly. Some members replicate the on-line coaching process and audiotape their consultation sessions for review with the IC-Team Facilitator serving as coach. Some members have the IC-Team Facilitator observe during an actual case consultation and notes are taken for later review. Still others identify permanent products (i.e., case documentation forms) that can be reviewed to determine application of skills. Finally, some members simply review orally their experience highlighting the specific targeted skills.

This data collection allows for the final step in the process, the coaching conference. The IC-Team Facilitator and team member review the data collected reflecting on the particular skill or area agreed to within the preconference stage. Unlike the technical coaching offered in the on-line component, the coaching conference is typically less directed by the coach and more of a shared reflection with the team member. Although participants have provided positive feedback regarding the supportive and comfortable nature of the on-site coaching, there remains a critical need to further investigate the impact of such a coaching model on the development of consultation skills.

IC Teaming as Continued Professional Development

In addition to individual coaching, IC-Team meetings are structured by the trained IC-Team Facilitator so individual consultants continue developing consultation skills through systematic training and case reviews. The facilitator schedules and conducts weekly 1-hour meetings and periodic daylong training sessions to develop and refine specific skills and knowledge introduced during the summer institute. By utilizing the various professional development methods outlined in Table 1 the IC-Team Facilitator strategically plans and delivers professional development activities to impact participants' acquisition and application of consultation skills.

The purpose of the team meeting remains twofold—supporting the progress of individual cases *and* ensuring that each team member continues to develop skills in consultation. Team meetings are structured to support the problem solving skills introduced within the institute with roles assigned to facilitate team development. In this instance the team process takes on a level of group coaching commonly cited in the literature (Garmston, 1987). In addition, team agendas and accompanying support materials provide on-going reinforcement of the specific skills associated with instructional consultation. Studies are currently underway to formally examine the process and outcome of IC teaming on members' professional development of consultation skills.

Roles.   Although there is some variation between sites, there is a defined structure and order of events that take place in a typical meeting. Teams have assigned key roles to specific members including facilitator, note taker, time keeper, case consultant, presenting teacher, and snack provider. Each role becomes crucial to the functioning and problem-solving integrity of the meetings. This distribution of labor serves to maintain focus of the meeting on the explicit goal of the meetings—problem solving of cases and as a mechanism for team members to further their development. As members rotate through the positions they acquire the skills associated with each, and are coached and supported by other members.

Agenda.   There is a specific agenda to the meetings rather than allowing for meetings to unfold in a haphazard manner. The structure sets the meeting as a social space in which the participants actively discuss, conceptualize and speculate about students' functioning as well as their own development of consultation skills. During early team development agendas also include opportunities for direct continuing education (i.e., CBA practice and introduction of reading interventions), discussion of team goals, and temperature taking (a structured process for team maintenance).

In support of the continued development of team members' skills, the agenda is structured to reinforce both the understanding and use of the problem-solving language on a weekly basis. For example, case updates are brief and require each member to report only their current stage of problem solving. This reinforcement of the problem-solving process is continued during the longest segment of the meeting in which cases are reviewed and discussed. At this time members often overtly continue their acquisition of skills and a refinement of their intellectual understanding of key concepts. Again, members are required to present cases according to the current stage of problem solving. However, the facilitator also conducts a brief review of that particular stage of problem solving, its key features and required tasks. Following the case presentation, the remaining team members are facilitated to provide support and feedback specific to the features and tasks required of the particular problem solving stage presented within the case review. This process serves to reinforce team members' understanding of the consultation process, and to maintain integrity of that process by not allowing members to overlook critical features relevant to the stage of problem solving. In this sense, structured case reviews during the team meeting serve as a technical coaching experience for the team member presenting the case, and as a training review for the remaining team members.

Instructional materials.   To ensure that the team stays focused and within the parameters of the IC problem solving process, some teams have created oversized posters displayed on walls. These posters contain information about the order of the problem solving process, communication strategies, and representations of critical IC concepts. Members have been observed to access the information on these posters as they engage in conversation about case progress and their own thinking related to the case and consultation.

In addition, some teams have extended the use of these recurrent team meetings as a vehicle for professional development in unexpected ways, such as videotaping or audiotaping consultation sessions for later study by the whole team. With the permission of consultants and teachers, the tapes are played during team meetings so that members have additional models of consultation within real-world settings as well as have the opportunity to provide feedback to the consultant regarding specific skill use and application.

In the IC-Team model members have to either acquire or adapt some very specific domains of knowledge: problem solving skills, effective communication skills, assessment, interventions and data collection techniques (Rosenfield & Gravois, 1996). These domains are not simply content-based, but in fact require members to use particular kinds of intra and interpersonal cognitive and social processes. The teaming structure of the meetings requires that participants create a shared understanding of what they are doing together, such that they are verbally and conceptually on the same page with one another. It is essential that members have the ability to interact within the structures of the IC-Teams and, for example, use the same coordinate principles and skills in problem solving (Rosenfield & Gravois, 1996). The individual presentations, demonstrations, and simulations that occur in each meeting, throughout the course of the school year, provide for an in situ forum for training and refinement of participants' problem solving skills.

SUMMARY

The primary goal of the IC-Team Consortium is to educate a diverse group of educational professionals as instructional consultants (Rosenfield, 1987, 2002) within the framework of IC-Teams (Rosenfield & Gravois, 1996). The major challenge faced in educating practitioners as consultants is the ability to create a continuum of professional development opportunities that effectively moves participants through skill development into accurate application. Of particular difficulty is the establishment of opportunities to receive either coaching or supervision during the application of introduced skills within the real-world setting. As described here, the IC-Team Consortium addresses this challenge by incorporating an intense, systematic staff development component (i.e., institute) followed by a structured coaching process (either on-site or on-line) and a focused teaming experience, all for the purpose of developing and enhancing practitioners' skills as instructional consultants. The IC-Team Consortium represents one method to create and sustain a comprehensive process for educating practitioners as consultants. The next step is to systematically evaluate the impact of this comprehensive training structure on the development of participants' consultations skills, and the degree to which such service delivery impacts both student and teacher performance.

REFERENCES

Anton, J. M., & Rosenfield, S. (2000, February). *A survey of preservice consultation training and supervision.* Poster session presented at the annual meeting of the National Association of School Psychologists, New Orleans.

Caccia, P. F. (1996). Linguistic coaching: Helping beginning teachers defeat discouragement. *Educational Leadership, 53,* 17–20.

Costenbader, V., Swartz, J., & Petrix, L. (1992). Consultation in the schools: The relationship between preservice training, perception of consultative skills, and actual time spent in consultation. *School Psychology Review, 21,* 95–108.

Fullan, M. (2001). *The new meaning of educational change.* New York: Teachers College Press.

Gallesich, J. (1983). Training psychologists for consultation with organizations. In J. L. Alpert & J. Meyers (Eds.), *Training in consultation: Perspectives form mental health, behavioral and organizational consultation* (pp. 142–163). Springfield, IL: Thomas.

Garmston, R. J. (1987). How administrators support peer coaching. *Educational Leadership, 44,* 18–26.

Goals 2000 Act. (1994). *Educate America Act,* Pub. L. No. 103–227.

Gravois, T. A., & Gickling, E. (2002). Best practices in curriculum based assessment. In A. Thomas & J. Grimes (Eds.), *Best practices in school psychology* (Vol. 4, pp. 885–898). Washington, DC: National Association of School Psychologists.

Gravois, T. A., Rosenfield, S., & Gickling, E. (1999). *IC-Team Training Manual.* Unpublished manuscript.

Gravois, T.A., Rosenfield, S., & Vail., (1999). Achieving effective and inclusive school settings: A guide for professional development. In S. Pfeiffer & L. Reddy (Eds.), *Inclusion practices with special needs students: Theory, research and application* (pp. 145–170). New York: Haworth Press.

Gutkin, T. B., & Curtis, M. J. (1982). School–based consultation: Theory and techniques. In C. R. Reynolds & T. B. Gutkin (Eds.), *The handbook of school psychology* (pp. 796–828). New York: Wiley.

Gutkin, T. B., & Curtis, M. J. (1999). School–based consultation theory and practice: The art and science of indirect service delivery. In C. R. Reynolds & T. B. Gutkin (Eds.), *The handbook of school psychology* (3rd ed., pp. 598–637). New York: Wiley.

Hawley, W.D., & Valli, L. (1999). The essentials of effective professional development. In L. Darling-Hammond & G. Sykes (Eds.), *Teaching as the learning profession: Handbook of policy and practice* (pp. 127–150). San Francisco: Jossey-Bass.

Idol, L. (1993). Preservice education and professional staff development. In J. E. Zins, T. R. Kratochwill, & S. N. Elliott (Eds.), *Handbook of consultation Service for children* (pp. 351–372). San Francisco: Jossey-Bass.

Idol, L., & West, J. F. (1987). Consultation in special education (Part II): Training and practice. *Journal of Learning Disabilities, 20,* 474–494.

Joyce, B., & Showers, B. (1980). Improving inservice training: The messages of research. *Educational Leadership, 37,* 379–385.

Kratochwill, T. R., Sheridan, S. M., Rotto, P. C., & Salmon, D. (1991). Preparation of school psychologists to serve as consultants for teachers of emotionally disturbed children. *School Psychology Review, 20,* 530–550.

Kratochwill, T. R., Sheridan, S. M., Rotto, P. C., & Salmon, D. (1992). Preparation of school psychologists in behavioral consultation service delivery. In T. R. Kratochwill & S. N. Elliott (Eds.), *Advances in school psychology* (Vol. 8, pp. 115–152). Hillsdale, NJ: Lawrence Erlbaum Associates, Inc.

Kruger, L. J., Cohen, S., Marca, D., & Matthews, L. (1996). Using the Internet to extend training in team problem solving. *Behavior Research Methods, Instruments, and Computers, 28,* 248–252.

Kruger, L. J., & Struzziero, J. (1997). Computer-mediated peer support of consultation: Case description and evaluation. *Journal of Educational and Psychological Consultation, 8,* 75–90.

Maxwell, L., & McCain, T. (1995). *Graduate distance education: A review and synthesis of the research literature.* Albuquerque, NM: Annual Conference of the International Communication Association (ERIC Document Reproduction Service No. ED 387118).

McDougall, L., Reschly, D. J., & Corkery, J. M. (1988). Changes in referral interviews with teachers after behavioral consultation training. *Journal of School Psychology, 26,* 225–232.

McMahon, T., Ward, N., Pruett, M., Davidson, L., & Griffith, E. (2000). Building full-servcie schools: Lessons learned in the development of interagency collaboratives. *Journal of Educational and Psychological Consultation, 11,* 65–92.

Myric, R., & Sabell, R. (1995). Cyberspace: A new place for counselor supervision. *Elementary School Guidance and Counseling, 30,* 35–44.

Reschly, D. J. (1993). A review of continuing education programs. In J. E. Zins, T. R. Kratochwill, & S. N. Ellicott (Eds.), *Handbook of consultation services for children* (pp. 351–372). San Francisco: Jossey-Bass.

Reschly, D. J. (2000). The present and future status of school psychology in the United States. *School Psychology Review, 29,* 507–522.

Reschly, D. J., & Wilson, J. E. (1995). School psychology practitioners and faculty: 1986 to 1991–92: Trends in demographics, roles, satisfaction, and system reform. *School Psychology Review, 24,* 62–80.

Rosenfield, S. (1987). *Instructional consultation.* Hillsdale, NJ: Lawrence Erlbaum Associates, Inc.

Rosenfield, S. (2002). Best practices in instructional consultation. In A Thomas & J. Grimes (Eds.), *Best practices in school psychology* (Vol. 4, pp. 609–623). Washington, DC: National Association of School Psychologists.

Rosenfield, S., & Gravois, T. A. (1996). *Instructional consultation teams: Collaborating for change.* New York: Guilford.

Rosenfield, S. & Gravois, T. A. (1999). Working with teams in the school. In C. Reynolds and T. Gutkin (Eds.), *Handbook of school psychology* (3rd ed., pp. 1025–1040). New York: Wiley.

Saxl, E., Lieberman, A., & Miles, M. (1987). Help is at hand: New knowledge for teachers and staff developers. *Journal of Staff Development, 8,* 7–11.

Showers, B., Joyce, B., & Bennett, B. (1987). Synthesis of research on staff development: A framework for future study and state-of-the-art analysis. *Educational Leadership, 45,* 77–87.

Showers, B., & Joyce, B. (1996). The evolution of peer coaching. *Educational Leadership, 53,* 12–16.

Spitzer, W., & Wedding, K. (1995). LabNet: An intentional electronic community for professional development. *Computers in Education, 24,* 247–255.

Vail, L., Gravois, T., & Rosenfield, S. (2001). *IC-Team facilitator training manual.* Unpublished manuscript.

Ysseldyke, J. E., Dawson, P., Lehr, C., Reschly, D., Reynolds, M., & Telzrow, C. (1997). *School psychology: A blueprint for training and practice II.* Bethesda, MD: National Association of School Psychologists.

Zins, J. E., Curtis, M. J., Graden, J. L., & Ponti, C. R. (1988). *Helping students succeed in the regular education classroom.* San Francisco: Jossey-Bass.

Zins, J. E., Elias, M. J., Greenberg, M. T., & Pruett, M. K. (Eds.). (2000). Implementation of prevention programs [Special issue]. *Journal of Educational and Psychological Consultation, 11*(1).

Todd A. Gravois is Research Associate and Co-director of the Laboratory for IC-Teams at the University of Maryland. His research and practice interests include training, implementation and evaluation of consultation-based services in schools, problem-solving teams and curriculum-based assessment.

Steve Knotek is an Assistant Professor of School Psychology at Bucknell University. His research interests include the process of consultation and collaboration within problem solving teams in schools, and the use of consultation as an intervention for promotion of minority students' success in regular education.

Leslie M. Babinski is an Assistant Professor and Director of the School Counseling Program in the Education Department at Bucknell University. Her research interests include new teacher groups, consultee-centered consultation, and risk and resiliency factors in children with ADHD. Along with Dwight Rogers, she has authored a new book on Teacher Groups called "From Isolation to Conversation" published by SUNY Press.

JOURNAL OF EDUCATIONAL AND PSYCHOLOGICAL CONSULTATION, 13(1&2), 133–146
Copyright © 2002, Lawrence Erlbaum Associates, Inc.

Training School-Based Consultants: Some Thoughts On Grains of Sand and Building Anthills

Terry B. Gutkin
San Francisco State University

This article reviews the major themes and issues emerging from this special issue on training school-based consultants. It is suggested that the building of anthills from individual and often seemingly disconnected grains of sand provides a useful metaphor for work in this arena. To date we have failed to establish a compelling and integrated body of empirical evidence addressing consultant training, although some excellent preliminary data have been reported. All agree that substantially more scholarly work is essential. It is proposed that the most important challenge facing us is the adoption of a unifying theoretical model to guide the organization and synthesis of our disparate "grains of sand" so that we can create meaningful and coherent "anthills" that can be of value to consultation trainers. Ecological and systems orientations are presented as the most appropriate and powerful approaches to achieve this goal. Small-N and qualitative research methodologies seem particularly well suited to this task. A number of specific research and practice ideas are suggested, although each has yet to garner sufficient empirical support and each is considered to be subsidiary to the adoption of an ecological paradigm to guide trainers and researchers in drafting a blueprint for future scientific work. As sure as worker ants can build phenomenally complex anthills from the most meager beginnings, so can we develop a scientific body of knowledge regarding consultant training. However, substantially more intellectual capital will need to be invested in this task if we are to succeed. Ultimately, it is up to us, as interested scholars, to make this happen.

Correspondence should be addressed to Terry B. Gutkin, College of Health and Human Services, 524 Burk Hall, Department of Counseling, 1600 Holloway Avenue, San Francisco, CA 94132. E-mail: tgutkin@sfsu.edu

I am pleased indeed to have this opportunity to comment on the articles in this special issue of the *Journal of Educational and Psychological Consultation* addressing the training of school-based consultants. Among the authors for this volume are many of the most outstanding thinkers, researchers, practitioners, and trainers in our field. Collectively, they have almost limitless wisdom and a century or more of experience pertinent to consulting in school settings and training others to follow in their footsteps. And yet, for all of this "firepower," one comes away from the articles in this special issue without any sense of closure. One underlying theme that permeates virtually all of the articles is that we lack the empirical research to answer many of our most basic training questions (e.g., how many graduate courses are needed for students to achieve competence, when in a student's training program should consultation theory and practice be taught, how should consultation courses be structured, how should students be supervised in field practice, where should field practice take place). Clearly, at this time, when it comes to training school-based consultants there are many more questions than answers.

One might presume that as the discussant for this special issue that I would be perturbed by this state of affairs. However, that is not the case. I can think of few meaningful questions in the social sciences that have been answered with certitude and finality. And even for those that have reached this lofty goal, the process of inquiry does not cease at that point. Rather, resolved questions simply and inevitably move us on to more sophisticated, powerful, and important questions. Such is the process of science and building increasingly complex bodies of knowledge.

All of which brings me to anthills. Even without being entomologists, we can all appreciate the sophistication, intricacy, and practicality of anthills. Although most of us spend little time thinking about such things, it is easy to see nonetheless that they truly are wondrous creations. They are examples of complex and highly functional systems that emerge from the most meager beginnings. When seen from this perspective, one can begin to glimpse the possibility that ants and anthills have something important to teach us as social scientists.

For one thing, every anthill starts as an unimpressive array of seemingly disconnected grains of sand. Those working on constructing the anthill, however, are not turned away from their task despite the daunting nature of what remains to be accomplished. Rather, at the risk of anthropomorphizing, I suspect they are energized to get on with the work at hand and build a structure that will someday meet the needs of their community, even if they do not know exactly what that structure will ultimately look like at the outset of the construction process. Moreover, each grain of sand placed on the anthill is relatively unimportant in and of itself. For it is not the individual grains of sand that make a difference, but rather the relationship among them that really matters. Being successful at building an anthill requires more than simply piling material on top of other material in a haphazard manner. The essential key to success is interconnecting each grain of sand with others in such a way as to create an organized, systemic entity that is far more than the sum of its individual parts.

Although seemingly far astray from training school-based consultants, I believe that the metaphorical anthill I've been describing can prove to be of considerable assistance as we evaluate the state of our knowledge and the value of this special issue.

IS THE ANTHILL WORTH BUILDING?

Obviously, not all anthills are worth building. Their creation requires time, effort, and the expenditure of a wide array of resources. The survival of an ant colony likely depends to a large extent on making good decisions regarding which anthills should be built and which are not worth the price of construction. In many ways, this is the most fundamental question we have to ask about the development of a scholarly literature pertaining to the training of school-based consultants. Is it a worthwhile undertaking? The existence of this special issue suggests that at least for the Editor of this journal, the Guest Editors for this special issue, and the authors contributing to this special issue, the answer would be "yes." This is not, however, as easy a question to answer as it might seem initially.

As illuminated by each of the articles in this special issue, building a valid body of scientific knowledge in the area of training school-based consultants has not been, and will never be, a simple task. Our field will have to expend substantially more intellectual capital if we are to reach a point of knowledge that is sufficient to inform daily practices. Are we willing and ready to do so? Although I would like to conclude otherwise, I must say that my reading of the extant literature as presented in this special issue (and my own knowledge of consultation research) suggests that as of 2002 our field has not demonstrated sufficient resolve in this regard. If it is true that the best predictor of future behavior is past behavior, one cannot be entirely sanguine about our own collective motivation to construct a science of training consultants.

Perhaps one critical restraint in producing a scholarly literature is that we have yet to discuss fully or resolve whether training consultants is an activity that should be guided primarily by science or art. The easy answer, of course, is that elements of both approaches are needed. Even though I accept this response as a truism, it doesn't really deal with the issue adequately. I suspect that there are many among us who do not perceive that science is the proper tool for developing and refining our training methodologies for consultants. Personally, I disagree with this position. Much as educational psychologists have been able to create a literature on effective teaching for children (Gettinger & Stoiber, 1999), we should be able to create and apply a science of consultant training. Regardless of my point of view on this matter, however, it is highly unlikely that such a science will come into being until a critical mass of consultant trainers concurs with the idea that consultant training can and should be driven largely by scientific insights. In effect, our belief that it is possible to create empirically based interventions (Kratochwill & Stoiber, 2000, in press; Stoiber & Kratochwill, 2000) needs to be extended to encompass the arena of consultant training as well as treatment protocols. Without this, I fear we will continue to be "professionally correct" in our writings, touting the value of science, but making no meaningful scientific progress.

Is this anthill worth building? I think so. However, much as a few scattered and disorganized grains of sand on the ground do not really lead to a "world class" anthill (if such a thing exists), the occasional article here and there (and even more occasional empirical study) also is likely to lead us nowhere that is truly productive. As every worker ant must know, building anthills requires sustained and organized effort. Even though I applaud everyone involved with this special issue, I know that at best it is but one small piece that ultimately must be built on by others that follow if it is to produce results of lasting value. At worst, it is just another isolated grain of sand lying on the ground that will never be part of a larger, meaningful whole. In the final analysis, it is up the *JEPC* readership and other interested scholars to determine whether the anthill gets built.

IS THE ANTHILL BEING BUILT?

If we analogize creating a scientific and professionally useful body of knowledge pertaining to training school-based consultants to building an anthill, how far have we come thus far? To date, how high is the anthill we've constructed? There is good news and bad news here, and both run deeply and pervasively throughout this special issue.

Beginning with the "bad news," virtually every author in this volume discusses the shortcomings of our extant literature. Alpert and Taufique (this issue) suggest that "in 1983, Alpert and Meyers indicated that there had been relatively little attention to consultation training in the literature. The situation has not changed much in the last 20 years." J. Meyers (this issue) argues, "that there is a compelling need for research investigating the process and outcomes of training in consultation." Despite discussing some examples to the contrary, Kratochwill and Pittman (this issue) characterize the consultation training literature as "too limited." Whether considering the uncertainties that face our longstanding "veterans" (Alpert and Taufique, this issue) or those relatively new to the field (A. Meyers, this issue), it is clear that many of the most fundamental questions regarding the training of school-based consultants have yet to be addressed satisfactorily in our scholarly literature. As of this date, nobody really knows how consultation skills can best be taught.

And yet there is "good news" to report as well. For one thing, both political power and scientific knowledge abhor a vacuum. Facing the existing limitations of our theory and data can only serve to stimulate further and increase meaningful work regarding the training of school-based consultants. This special issue, as such, is part of the solution and helps to provide the foundation on which our anthill is going to be built. It both raises the essential questions we need to address in the future and begins to provide some answers as well. Every article in this issue has important ideas to share with its readers. From the set of articles as a whole one comes away with an array of possibilities for one's own training practices and future research agendas, whether they be for preservice (Alpert & Taufique, this issue; A. Meyers, this issue; Rosenfield, this issue) or inservice (Gravois, Knotek, & Babinski, this issue) work. Although the personal experiences and case studies found in this special issue are not the grains of sand that will complete our anthill, they are among those that will help us form a foundation and start to make meaningful progress in the building process.

It is also important to note that concurrent with this special issue, some meaningful and comprehensive empirical work has been, and is being, done in the area of training school-based consultants. Kratochwill and Pittman (this issue) discuss much of this research base (e.g., Kratochwill, Elliott, & Busse, 1995; Lepage, Kratochwill, & Elliott, in press), which is noteworthy because it assesses comprehensive outcomes of consultation training on clients, consultees (e.g., teachers, parents), and consultants, and includes both objective measures of client progress (e.g., direct observations of behavior change) and subjective assessment of consultation outcomes (e.g., goal attainment scaling, intervention acceptability measures). Parallel research training teachers to be effective collaborative, problem solvers is reported by Allen and Blackston (in press).

Is the anthill being built? Once again I would answer in the affirmative. While not denying that we are at the very early stages of this construction effort, we have, nonetheless, broken ground and started to organize our foundational grains of sand on which the larger structure will stand ultimately. Like every anthill, we have to start somewhere. I believe we have made that start. Counterbalancing my optimism is the reality that If we fail to continue advancing forward, we have little, if anything, as of this date that would stand the test of time. Partially constructed foundations are not of great value in and of themselves. They are worthy only to the extent that they provide a platform on which we can build further.

SELECTED KEYS TO IMPROVING
THE EXISTING ANTHILL

This brings us to the really difficult questions. How do we go from a rudimentary foundation to creating a fully built and functioning anthill? Although a complete response to this "big" question is beyond the limited scope of this response article, I would suggest that we consider how anthills get built to gain at least some useful guidance. Doing so makes a few points obvious. First, this is not a one-person job. It will take a considerable number of us willing to devote ourselves to the task at hand. In addition, like the ants themselves, we are unlikely to be successful if we work in an uncoordinated manner. That is, although we need not have a "conductor," like a great orchestra, we do need some sort of plan that each worker ant accepts and follows. I would suggest that this plan is the scientific process itself. We must each be cognizant of, and building on, the grains of sand that are placed on the anthill prior to our own. Our research work must add to and extend that which has preceded it. Just stacking "stuff" up willy-nilly will not lead to a coherent outcome.

Perhaps providing one terse example can help illustrate the anthill building process to which I am alluding. In Caplan's classic work (1970), he underscored the importance of collaboration, but provided no clear definition of this complex construct and suggested no empirical methodology for assessing its presence or absence. Shortly thereafter, Bergan (1977) fleshed out this central consultative element by providing a measure, the Consultation Analysis Record (CAR), with which consultant and consultee behaviors could be assessed. Even though the collaborative construct was far from fully delineated, the CAR provided a starting point from which to examine empirically its presence or absence during consultation interactions. This instrument was modified slightly and used precisely for this purpose by Gutkin (1996), who found numerous empirical findings supporting collaborative processes during consultation interviews. Erchul and his colleagues (Erchul, 1987; Erchul & Chewning, 1990; Witt, Erchul, McKee, Pardue, & Wickstrom, 1991) argued however that the CAR was fundamentally flawed because it focused individually on consultant and consultee behaviors and failed to pay sufficient attention to the interactions between their verbalizations. To advance our knowledge they employed relational measures (e.g., topic determination, dominant-submissive bids), which analyzed the give-and-take between consultants and consultees, and concluded that consultation was not a collaborative enterprise in the sense in which it had previously been described. Gutkin (1999b) responded by re-analyzing the data presented by Erchul and his colleagues and suggesting that their conclusions were faulty. More important, Gutkin suggested a new methodology for assessing collaboration by distinguishing collaborative and directive behaviors as distinctive rather than opposite ends of the same continuum. Erchul (1999) responded to Gutkin's model and Gutkin (1999a) subsequently responded to Erchul's remarks. Most recently, Sheridan, Meegan, and Eagle (2002) have employed the Psychosocial Process Coding Scheme (Leaper, 1991) to add yet more grains onto this growing anthill by modifying the conceptual model suggested by Gutkin (1999b). Their latest work provides a highly operationalized definition of collaboration, and suggests that collaborative and obliging interactions between consultants and consultees are the predominant relational style in effective conjoint consultation cases.

Presenting this sequence of works is not intended to imply that we have reached an end point and that our proverbial anthill has been completed. Without doubt, that is not the case. There is more to come (I hope) as our body of knowledge grows and develops. Rather this series of investigations and articles is intended to illustrate an ongoing example of anthill building and the clear benefits it can yield. Although not directly connected to consultant training per se, there can be no doubt that exploring the construct of collaboration and how it can be measured has substantive implications for how we train students to function effectively as consultants. More important, the process of extending scientific knowledge is the same, regardless of whether one is looking at providing consultation services or training school-based consultants.

Taking this perspective leads to a point of great importance. Someone much smarter than I once said, "There is nothing more practical than good theory." Although I do not recall the author of this sage advice, it is central to how great bodies of scientific knowledge are built. Clearly, not all things that are accessible to ants are of equal value when constructing an anthill. Some materials are better than others because they fit more effectively with, and add to, the existing structure. As scientists we know that not all data are of equal value. Some are more relevant than others as we attempt to construct an organized body of information. The value of a good theory is that it helps guide us as individual researchers to ask relevant questions, which can be addressed via research and practice.

Is there a particular theoretical perspective that is of special value for trainers and researchers as we attempt to build a science of consultation training? No doubt the answer is "yes." Which theory that is may well be a personal preference. Nonetheless, as I read through this special issue I was struck by the fact that each and every author made either direct or at least indirect reference to ecological/systems theory. As one might guess from my own prior writings (e.g., Gutkin & Conoley, 1990; Sheridan & Gutkin, 2000), I see this as a critical perspective for the provision of effective consultation training and service provision.

What I perceive as the inherent value of ecological theory is that it focuses our efforts on interconnected contexts rather than simply on the pathology of presenting clients. If we are to train students, teachers, etc. on a preservice or inservice basis to be effective consultants, it will be essential to attend to the interpersonal, organizational, family and community contexts within which consultation cases present themselves. In my estimation, this is an inescapable conclusion that any fair-minded reader would reach after perusing this special issue. There are many superb examples of this, including, but not limited to: (a) Rosenfield's (this issue) focus on the centrality of relationship building and understanding how consultees construct meaning from the way we, as consultants, employ language; (b) J. Meyers' (this issue) view of consultation and consultation training within the context of constructivism, in which the meaning of communication is created by subjective perceptions of listeners; (c) A. Meyers' (this issue) examination of how Black feminist epistemology could be employed to build collaboration despite power differentials in consultant-consultee relationships; (d) Kratochwill and Pittman's (this issue) discussion of involving parents and peers in consultation processes, in addition to teachers and related school personnel; (e) Gravois et al.'s (this issue) consideration of consultation services within the context of team and organizational dynamics in schools; and (f) Alpert and Taufique's (this issue) compelling presentation of how the culture of one particular school impacted dramatically the handling of sensitive and explosive issues presented in a consultation case, and how the daily realities of all schools must be examined when considering the nature of placements and supervision for consultation training. Attempting to boil all these important issues down into a meaningful brief phrase, I try to communicate to my students that "context counts."

Choosing ecological/systems theory as a central organizing theme for training school-based consultants allows us to stay focused on context, that is the multivariate and multi-level systems that surround each and every consultation case. Going back to our anthill metaphor, it lets scholars know what type of "stuff" is needed to strengthen and expand on the anthill we've developed thus far to date and it lets trainers know what kinds of experiences students will likely need to develop into competent consultants.

Regarding the former, ecological perspectives suggest that univariate research designs focusing on decontexualized client (e.g., DSM & IDEA diagnoses) or consultee (e.g., years of teaching experience) characteristics are unlikely to advance our knowledge base very effectively. Rather, research strategies that address the multivariate contexts of consultation practice would seem to hold considerably more promise. Consultation training, processes and outcomes must be examined simultaneously through the eyes of consultants, consultees, clients, and client systems. Small-N and qualitative designs would appear to be particularly well suited for this task because they allow us to examine the unique ecological complexities of each individual case. Research by Lepage et al. (in press) and Allen and Blackston (in press) demonstrated the potential of the small-N approach, while Truscott, Cosgrove, Meyers, and Eidle-Barkman (2000) and Athanasiou, Geil, Hazel, and Copeland (2002) provided evidence of the important contributions that can be made by qualitative methodologies. The works by Lepage et al., and Allen and Blackston are of particular relevance to this special issue as they focus explicitly on consultation training per se.

Regarding the latter, ecological perspectives suggest that in vivo, field-based work is the ultimate key to training competent consultants. In light of the contextualized complexities of actual practice, however, it would seem unwise to initiate training at that point. Rather, students would likely prosper from practice and mastery along a continuum of increasingly complex consultation skills. These might begin with building knowledge (e.g., intervention design) and isolated micro-consultation abilities (e.g., active listening) via didactic presentations, role plays, etc. and conclude with live, supervised practice in field settings. Given the ecological complexity of typical consultation cases, it is probably unrealistic to expect our students to become competent consultants with only 1–2 courses and minimal supervision under their belt (although surveys [e.g., Costenbader, Swartz, & Petrix, 1992] suggest that this typifies contemporary consultation training in graduate programs). A central point for the purposes of this article, however, is that although I believe each of the above propositions to be true, I have far too little empirical data to determine whether my beliefs are accurate. Again, the need for more research in the area of training school-based consultants is clear. My primary point here is that ecological theory will assist us in determining what research questions are most worthy if we wish to develop a science of consultant training.

Above and beyond viewing consultation training and research through an ecological/systems prism, a number of additional and critical unifying themes emerge clearly from this special issue. Space limitations prevent an extensive analysis of these points, but they are also too important to ignore entirely. Like the ecological model, these themes help us know what is relevant as we attempt to advance our scholarly knowledge and practice regarding the training of school-based consultants. They help us have a plan for building our metaphorical anthill, rather than proceeding in a haphazard manner.

Perhaps most important is the idea that consultation revolves around interpersonal processes *and* problem solving. Students must be competent in both domains. They must learn how to establish and maintain effective relationships with their consultees, while also helping consultees solve their problems. These are distinct domains of competence and it would seem unwise to assume that skillful behavior in one area assures high levels of achievement in the other. Logically, training programs must devote considerable emphasis in both areas to produce competent school-based consultants.

Another critical point to emerge, particularly from the articles by Gravois et al. (this issue) and J. Meyers (this issue), is the fact that so much school-based consultation currently takes place in groups (Gutkin & Nemeth, 1999), such as teacher support and prereferral intervention teams, rather than in one-on-one contexts. Despite this, it is my clear sense that only a very small portion of our research and training focuses on group consultation. Clearly, additional skills are needed for group work and failing to train students in these areas leaves them highly vulnerable to failure and ineffective service delivery. As shown by a number of studies, group consultation often can be very effective when it is done properly (e.g., Nelson, Smith, Taylor, Dodd, & Reavis, 1991), but often is practiced inappropriately and thus leads to poor outcomes (e.g., Flugum & Reschly, 1994; Meyers, Valentino, Meyers, Boretti, & Brent, 1996; Wilson, Gutkin, Hagen, & Oats, 1998). If we continue to ignore this training agenda, we do so at our own peril. Assuming that group consultation will continue to grow in the future as the mandate for teacher support and prereferral intervention teams expands, current training practices must be refocused to attend much more heavily on group work.

Finally, I would like to underscore the value of what J. Meyers (this issue) refers to as the practitioner researcher model. I see this as closely related to concepts proposed for school psychologists, behavioral psychologists, and educators, respectively, by Stoner and Green (1992), Hayes, Barlow, and Nelson, (1999), and Reagan, Case, and Brubacher (2000). Each of these works suggests that practitioners should be practicing as reflective researchers as they function in their daily work. These approaches allow science and practice truly to inform each other. Teaching the science and practice of consultation in isolation from each other, as we typically do now, will do little to help build the body of knowledge we seek to construct. Given that it is the worker ants who are out in the field actually constructing the anthill, it would be a clear step forward if these "little buggers" would evaluate the quality of the anthill as they were building it. Although I suspect that most of our training programs have a long way to go before achieving this goal, it is an excellent target for all of us who train school-based consultants. As suggested by the ecological model, it is precisely those individuals who are immersed in the natural context in which services are offered who are in the best position to know what does and does not work, both for practice and training.

Of course, there are innumerable pressing research agendas pertaining to the training of consultants that were neither pervasive foci for this special issue nor addressed in this article (see Gutkin & Curtis, 1999, for a small list). In the final analysis, however, I always return to the underlying conceptualization(s) that should be driving our research projects. For me, these are more important than the individual research questions that we ask. As I've tried to argue in this article, an ecological orientation, if used appropriately, can serve as a blueprint, telling us: (a) which grains of sand we should lift and carry to the anthill and which to leave unattended, and (b) how to integrate discrete grains of sand so that together they form a coherent and meaningful whole. In a recent study I conducted with a colleague on treatment acceptability (Gray & Gutkin, 2001), the ecological model guided us to assess this construct across teachers, parents, administrators *and* students, hypothesizing that only interventions that were acceptable to *all* of these constituencies would be effective in the long run. Although far from a perfect study, it does provide a glimpse into how theory, in this case ecological theory, can (and should) guide the framing of research questions. In the end, I believe it is meaningful theory that will allow us to make progress. Without it, each individual grain of sand will remain precisely that and little else. Despite lots of hard work and grains of sand being carried hither and yon, the anthill itself will elude us.

CLOSING THOUGHTS

If ants can build anthills, we can build a rich and competent body of knowledge on how to train school-based consultants. While this might look like an unmanageable challenge at this point in our history, think of what building an anthill must look like to those workers that carry the first few grains of sand to the beginning construction site. Surely, our job must be easier than theirs. Perhaps most important, those ants that are unsuccessful at building an anthill to house their community are certain to perish. Although our lives obviously are not at stake, the probabilities of achieving our professional goals do, in fact, hang in the balance. To date we have not yet built our anthill and our graduates largely remain mired in a refer-test-place service delivery system. These events are not independent of each other. To change the latter, we will have to build the former. This special issue of the *Journal of Educational and Psychological Consultation* is a wonderful step forward and hopefully serves as a catalyst to energize trainers, practitioners and researchers alike. I challenge everyone reading this issue to lift up a grain of sand, figure out exactly how it fits with all the others that have been put in place before yours, and then add yours to the pile such that our scholarly anthill is just a bit better after you left it than before you found it.

REFERENCES

Allen, S. J., & Blackston, A. R. (in press). Training preservice teachers in collaborative problem solving: An investigation of the impact on teacher and student behavior change in real-world settings. *School Psychology Quarterly.*

Athanasiou, M. S., Geil, M., Hazel, C. E., & Copeland, E. P. (2002). A look inside school-based consultation: A qualitative study of the beliefs and practices of school psychologists and teachers. *School Psychology Quarterly, 17,* 258–298.

Bergan, J. R. (1977). *Behavioral consultation.* Columbus, OH: Merrill.

Caplan, G. (1970). *The theory and practice of mental health consultation.* New York: Basic Books.

Costenbader, V., Swartz, J., & Petrix, L. (1992). Consultation in the schools: The relationship between preservice training, perception of consultative skills, and actual time spent in consultation. *School Psychology Review, 21,* 210–221.

Erchul, W. P. (1987). A relational communication analysis of control in school consultation. *Professional School Psychology, 2,* 113–124.

Erchul, W. P. (1999). Two steps forward, one step back: Collaboration in school-based consultation. *Journal of School Psychology, 37,* 191–203.

Erchul, W. P., & Chewning, T. G. (1990). Behavioral consultation from a request-centered relational communication perspective. *School Psychology Quarterly, 5,* 1–20.

Flugum, K. R., & Reschly, D. J. (1994). Prereferral interventions: Quality indices and outcomes. *Journal of School Psychology, 32,* 1–14.

Gettinger, M., & Stoiber, K. C. (1999). Excellence in teaching: Review of instructional and environmental variables. In C. R. Reynolds & T. B. Gutkin (Eds.), *The handbook of school psychology* (3rd ed., pp. 933–958). New York: Wiley.

Gray, C. L. & Gutkin, T. B. (2001). Acceptability of rewards among high school teachers, parents, students and administrators: Ecological implications for consultation at the high school level. *Journal of Educational and Psychological Consultation, 12,* 25–43.

Gutkin, T. B. (1996). Patterns of consultant and consultee verbalizations: Examining communication leadership during initial consultation interviews. *Journal of School Psychology, 34,* 199–219.

Gutkin, T. B. (1999a). The collaboration debate: Finding our way through the maze: Moving forward into the future: A response to Erchul (1999). *Journal of School Psychology, 37,* 229–241.

Gutkin, T. B. (1999b). Collaborative versus directive/prescriptive/expert school-based consultation: Reviewing and resolving a false dichotomy. *Journal of School Psychology, 37,* 161–190.

Gutkin, T. B., & Conoley, J. C. (1990). Reconceptualizing school psychology from a service delivery perspective: Implications for practice, training, and research. *Journal of School Psychology, 28,* 203–223.

Gutkin, T. B., & Curtis, M. J. (1999). School-based consultation theory and practice: The art and science of indirect service delivery. In C. R. Reynolds & T. B. Gutkin (Eds.), *The handbook of school psychology* (3rd ed., pp. 598–637). New York: Wiley.

Gutkin, T. B., & Nemeth, C. (1997). Selected factors impacting decision making in prereferral intervention and other school-based teams: Exploring the intersection between school and social psychology. *Journal of School Psychology, 35,* 195–216.

Hayes, S. C., Barlow, D. H., & Nelson, R. O. (1999). *The scientist practitioner: Research and accountability in the age of managed care* (2nd ed.). Needham Heights, MA: Allyn & Bacon.

Kratochwill, T. R., Elliott, S. N., & Busse, R. T. (1995). Behavioral consultation: A five-year evaluation of consultant and client outcomes. *School Psychology Quarterly, 10,* 87–117.

Kratochwill, T. R., & Stoiber, K. C. (2000). Empirically supported interventions and school psychology: Conceptual and practical issues - Part II. *School Psychology Quarterly, 15,* 233–253.

Kratochwill, T. R., & Stoiber, K. S. (in press). Evidence-based interventions in school psychology: Conceptual foundations of the Procedural and Coding Manual of Division 16 and the Society for the Study of School Psychology Task Force. *School Psychology Quarterly.*

Leaper, C. (1991). Influence and involvement in children's discourse: Age gender and partner effects. *Child Development, 62,* 797–811.

Lepage, K., Kratochwill, T. R., & Elliott, S N. (in press). Competency-based behavior consultation training: An evaluation of consultant outcomes, treatment effects, and consumer satisfaction. *School Psychology Quarterly.*

Meyers, B., Valentino, C. T., Meyers, J., Boretti, B., & Brent, D. (1996). Implementing prereferral intervention teams as an approach to school-based consultation in an urban school system. *Journal of Educational and Psychological Consultation, 7,* 119–149.

Nelson, J. R., Smith, D. J., Taylor, L., Dodd, J. M., & Reavis, K. (1991). Prereferral intervention: A review of the research. *Education and Treatment of Children, 14,* 243–253.

Reagan, T. G., Case, C. W., & Brubacher, J. W. (2000). *Becoming a reflective education: How to build a culture of inquiry in the schools* (2nd ed.). Thousand Oaks, CA: Corwin Press.

Sheridan, S. M., & Gutkin, T. B. (2000). The ecology of school psychology: Examining and changing our paradigm for the 21st century. *School Psychology Review, 29,* 485–502.

Sheridan, S. M., Meegan, S. P., & Eagle, J. W. (2002). Assessing the social context in initial conjoint behavioral consultation interviews: An exploratory analysis investigating processes and outcomes. *School Psychology Quarterly, 17,* 299–324.

Stoiber, K. C., & Kratochwill, T. R. (2000). Empirically supported interventions and school psychology: Rationale and methodological issues - Part I. *School Psychology Quarterly, 15,* 75–115.

Stoner, G., & Green, S. K. (1992). Reconsidering the scientist–practitioner model for school psychology practice. *School Psychology Review, 21,* 155–166.

Truscott, S. D., Cosgrove, G., Meyers, J., & Eidle-Barkman, K. A. (2000). The acceptability of organizational consultation with prereferral intervention teams. *School Psychology Quarterly, 15,* 172–206.

Wilson, C. P., Gutkin, T. B., Hagen, K. M., & Oats, R. G. (1998). General education teachers' knowledge and self-reported use of classroom interventions for working with difficult-to-teach students: Implications for consultation, prereferral intervention and inclusive services. *School Psychology Quarterly, 13,* 45–62.

Witt, J. C., Erchul, W. P., McKee, W. T., Pardue, M. M., & Wickstrom, K. F. (1991). Conversational control in school-based consultation: The relationship between consultant and consultee topic determination and consultation outcome. *Journal of Educational and Psychological Consultation, 2,* 101–116.

Terry B. Gutkin received his doctorate from the University of Texas at Austin in 1975 in Educational Psychology with a specialization in school psychology. After serving on the School Psychology faculty for 26 years at the University of Nebraska-Lincoln, he now Chairs the Department of Counseling at San Francisco State University.

CONTRIBUTOR INFORMATION

Content: The *Journal of Educational and Psychological Consultation* (*JEPC*) provides a forum for improving the scientific understanding of consultation and for describing practical strategies to increase the effectiveness and efficiency of consultation services. Consultation is broadly defined as a process that facilitates problem solving for individuals, groups, and organizations. *JEPC* publishes articles and special thematic issues that describe formal research, evaluate practice, examine the program implementation process, review relevant literature, investigate systems change, discuss salient issues, and carefully document the translation of theory into practice. Examples of topics of interest include individual, group, and organizational consultation; collaboration; community-school-family partnerships; consultation training; educational reform; ethics and professional issues; health promotion; personnel preparation; preferral interventions; prevention; program planning, implementation, and evaluation; school to work transitions; services coordination; systems change; and teaming. Of interest are manuscripts that address consultation issues relevant to clients of all age groups, from infancy to adulthood. Manuscripts that investigate and examine how culture, language, gender, race, ethnicity, religion, and exceptionality influence the process, content, and outcome of consultation are encouraged. *JEPC* publishes empirical investigations as well as qualitative studies that use methodologies such as case studies and ethnography.

In addition to publishing research and theoretical articles, *JEPC* publishes three special columns. The **Consultant's Corner** column provides a forum for papers that explore new ideas or discuss content areas that are of interest to consultants. The **Diversity in Consultation** column features articles that examine the process of consultation within the context of human diversity. The **Book and Material Reviews** column features reviews of books and other professional materials (e.g., software programs, training modules) relevant to the process of consultation.

JEPC is dedicated to service a wide, interdisciplinary audience. Included among its readers are university-based and field-based personnel in the areas of clinical, community, counseling, organizational and school psychology; counselor education; educational administration; general, special, and remedial education; reading; social work; special services; speech and language pathology; and special services.

Manuscript Preparation: The Editor welcomes inquiries from authors about ideas for manuscripts and special issues. Authors of empirical treatment studies are asked to include information regarding the quality of the implementation process and about intervention fidelity. Papers describing qualitative investigations should carefully document procedures for data collection and data analyses. Authors are expected to discuss the practical significance of their findings using effect size indicators and/or narrative analyses. Manuscripts must address implications for the practice of consultation by a broad, interdisciplinary audience. Manuscripts should be prepared according to the Publication Manual of the American Psychological Association (APA; 5th edition). Type all components of the manuscript double-spaced, including title page, abstract, text quotes, acknowledgments, references, appendices, tables, figure captions, and footnotes. The abstract should be 100-150 words in length. A dot matrix or unusual typeface is acceptable only if it is clear and legible. To enable authors to address their topics comprehensively, manuscript of up to 35 pages of text (excluding references, tables, and figures) will be considered.

Manuscript Submission: In a cover letter, authors should state that they have complied with APA ethical standards in the treatment of their subjects, and that the manuscript is original, has not been previously published, and is not simultaneously being submitted to another journal. To facilitate anonymous review by members of the Editorial Board, each copy of the manuscript should include a separate title page with authors' names, affiliations, and an introductory footnote with the mailing and E-mail address of the corresponding author. This information should not appear anywhere else in the manuscript. It is the authors' responsibility to make every effort to see that the manuscript itself contains no clue as to their identities. Authors should supply their addresses; phone and fax numbers; and electronic mail addresses for potential use by the editorial and production offices. For additional details pertaining to manuscript submissions, visit www.erlbaum.com (click on journals and find *JEPC*).

Guidelines for submission of research and theoretical articles: Five copies of each manuscript should be submitted to Emilia C. Lopez; Editor; Queens College, CUNY; Educational and Community Programs; 65-30 Kissena Blvd., Flushing, NY 11367; 718-997-5234; lopez@cedx.com; Fax: 718-997-5248.

Guidelines for submission of Special Issues: To receive the guidelines for special issues, please contact Kathleen C. Harris, PhD, *JEPC* Associate Editor for Special Issues, College of Education, Arizona State University West, 4701 W. Thunderbird Road, P.O. Box 37100, Phoenix, AZ 85069-7100; 602-543-6339; kathleen.harris@asu.edu; Fax: 602-543-6350.

Column manuscripts vary in content and length and prospective authors should contact the column editors as follows. **The Consultant's Corner Column:** Margaret R. Rogers, PhD; Psychology Department; University of Rhode Island; Woodward 16; Kingston, RI 02881; 401-874-7999; mrogres@uri.edu; Fax: 401-874-2157. **Diversity in Consultation Column:** Mary M. Clare, PhD; MSC 86, Counseling Psychology; Lewis & Clark College; Portland, OR 97219; 503-768-6069; henning@lclark.edu; Fax: 503-768-6065. **Book and Material Reviews Column:** Emilia C. Lopez; Editor; Queens College, CUNY; Educational and Community Programs; 65-30 Kissena Blvd., Flushing, NY 11367; 718-997-5234; lopez@cedx.com; Fax: 718-997-5248. Authors who are interested in having books or materials reviewed should forward them to Dr. Lopez.

Review Policy: All manuscripts submitted for consideration as regular articles are mask reviewed. Reviews typically are completed within 3 months of submission, with the revision process (as needed) taking additional time.

Permissions: Authors are responsible for all statements made in their work and for obtaining permission from copyright owners to reprint or adapt a table or figure or to reprint a quotation of 500 words or more. Authors should write to original author(s) and publisher(s) to request nonexclusive world rights in all languages to use the material in the article and in future editions. Copies of all permissions and credit lines obtained must be provided prior to publication.

Publication Policy: Authors of research reports are expected to have available their data throughout the editorial review process and for 5 years following publication.

Production Notes: After a manuscript is accepted for publication, its author is asked to provide a computer disk containing the manuscript file. Files are copyedited and typeset into page proofs. Authors read proofs to correct errors and answer editors' queries. Authors receive a complementary copy of the issue in which their article appears, and they may order reprints of their articles only when they receive page proofs.